MW01617308

African Americans Aging
in the Rural South

Previous Books Published by the Author

African American Leadership: An Empowerment Tradition in Social Welfare History 2001(edited) National Association of Social Workers Press

Preserving and Strengthening Small Towns and Rural Communities 1999
(Edited with Richard Edwards & P. Nelson Reid)
National Association of Social Workers Press

African American Community Practice Models: Historical and Contemporary Responses 1996
(Edited with N. Yolanda Burwell)
Haworth Press, Inc.

African Americans Aging in the Rural South

Stories of Faith, Family and Community

Iris B. Carlton-LaNey, Ph.D.

Sourwood
Press, Inc.

Copyright © 2005 by Iris Carlton-LaNey

Carlton-LaNey, Iris. "The Last Quilting Bee," Reprinted with permission from **Generations**, 17:2, 55-58. Spring/Summer 1993 American Society on Aging, San Francisco, California. www.asaging.org

Carlton-LaNey, Iris. "Stories from Rural Elderly African Americans," Excerpt reprinted with permission from **Generations**, 27:3, 34-38. Fall 2003 American Society on Aging, San Francisco, California www.asaging.org

Carlton-LaNey, Iris, Elderly Black farm women: A population at risk," **Copyright 1992, National Association of Social Workers, Inc., Social Work**

Carlton-LaNey, Iris, **Elderly Black farm women as Keepers of the Community and the Culture. Copyright 1989** Appletex, Greensboro, NC.

All rights reserved. No part of this publication may be reproduced, stored in a retrieval system, or transmitted, in any form or by any means, electronic, mechanical, photocopying, recording, or otherwise, without the prior permission of Sourwood Press, Inc. (Iris Carlton-LaNey & Associates).

ISBN: 0-9771450-0-X

Cover Design: Miki Kersgard
Photographer: Marion L. LaNey, II
Cover Photograph: Ninety-two year old Duplin County, NC resident

To Mama
Annette Robinson Carlton

and her sister-friends

Acknowledgement

I am most grateful to the women who shared their stories, time and commitment, thus enabling me to complete this book. They are so dear to me, and I owe them immeasurably. I am indebted to my sister Sandra Carlton Alexander, who always reviews my work, has faith in my abilities and never fails to encourage me. I greatly appreciate my husband, Marion L. LaNey, II, for the photographs that grace these pages. I also want to acknowledge the many eyes that painstakingly read this book before it went to press especially my sister-in-law, Mary Ann Carlton, my colleague Sharon Holmes and my nieces, Tonya Alexander and Jessica Carlton. I appreciate Cindy McCorkle who helped me to remember the importance of a glossary. Many thanks also to others who took time to help me. Thank you Adeline Williams, Renee Askew, Gladys Dunston, Arnold Dennis, and Vanessa Hodges. A special acknowledgement is reserved for Marion L. LaNey, III (Donnie), my son, who is my joy.

Contents

Preface

This book is divided into three distinct but integrally connected parts. It is based on interviews with elderly African American farm women along with a lifetime of observing these women and men in their everyday surroundings and, finally, on the participant observation of a social work researcher who grew up in a small southeastern North Carolina community.

The setting, a small bucolic farming community, was inhabited by the descendants of two brothers who were enslaved for the first twelve to fifteen years of their lives. They inherited the land from their father who had purchased it two years after the Emancipation Proclamation was issued. The land was passed from fathers to sons and is affectionately named Carltontown, from the men's family name. Carltontown is a proud community of landholding farmers located six miles outside of the closest incorporated town. The community is known for its hardworking, independent and principled residents. This extended family network sustained itself over the years through self-help, communal work, worship, mutual aid and social support.

Part I is a collection of vignettes that I have written over a six year period. The vignettes describe events and activities of the Carltontown community illustrating the community's well-organized everyday lifestyle of the 1940s, 1950s, 1960s, and early 1970s. With virtually no embellishment, the vignettes are my interpretation of life in Carltontown as I experienced and observed it. Because I used these elderly women and men's voices wherever possible, some readers may find a glossary helpful in understanding some of the terminology of these rural elderly residents. To that end, a brief glossary is included at the back of the book and words in the text that are defined in the glossary are written in **bold**.

Part II contains interviews with ten elderly farm women from Carltontown, and a neighboring community, who ranged in age from 69 to 78. This section presents these women's stories in their own voices. It seemed important to use direct quotes for this section to ensure the veracity of their stories and to make certain that the stories were told the way that the women would have them be told. It is also critical to note that the women *trusted* me with their stories.

After a three hour candid and heartfelt interview with one of the women, she concluded with a cautionary note saying, "You know how much of this to use, don't you?" This statement, though in the form of a question, was her way of giving me the permission and responsibility to edit her story in a way that would protect both privacy and dignity. I took their trust seriously which made me both vigilant and honorable in reporting on their lives.

Part III includes two articles that were published in social work journals. The articles are based on the interviews from *Part II* and are intended to assist social workers and others in helping professions to better understand and work with these women and others like them. The content of these two articles could describe any rural, close-knit community of African American inhabitants and provides strategies for developing services and programs to meet their needs and to enhance the quality of their lives.

Readers will find *African Americans Aging in the Rural South* valuable in many different ways. It is written in a clear straightforward fashion and offers the reader an entertaining and educational glimpse of a small rural farming community of elderly women and men.

This book is first and foremost a document to honor the women and men who helped to develop this country and who modeled family strengths, charity and tenacity. Further, it helps to preserve the history of this particular group of people. It helps us to have a better understanding of the meaning of family in these rural communities from the pre-Depression years to the early 1970s. The book also gives us a unambiguous understanding of how African American families strategized for survival, provided motivation and designed inclusive kinship networks.

African Americans Aging in the Rural South also leaves a legacy for African American youth to build upon and emulate. That legacy is one of strength in the face of adversity and grace in times of trial. It's a legacy that illustrates resourcefulness and coping when exclusionary practices made it difficult, at best, to compete in American society. Yet these elders have contributed significantly to the overall American culture and recall their lives with pride, purpose and a sense of accomplishment.

This book can be used by social workers and health care providers, along with scholars in women studies, history and rural sociology, to better develop services, programs and policies that meet the needs of this oftentimes invisible population in American society.

The vignettes can be used to stimulate reminiscence or life review among elders, individually and in groups. These stories of rural life spanning over four decades can provide historians with primary data to further understand and record the history of rural African Americans. For classroom exercises, the novice and the seasoned teacher alike, can use this book to bring freshness and inspiration to teaching and learning about diversity, human behavior, aging and life in the rural south. Furthermore, this book can bring new insight and stimulate discussion in classrooms while deepening students' understanding of and respect for an important segment of the nation's elderly population.

Finally, I encourage the reader to share this book with others. Read it to children, at family reunions, for church groups, etc. Read it wherever these elders' voices can bring a smile, a comforting sigh of remembrance or simply an affirmative nod of understanding and appreciation for a job well done and a life well spent.

*P*art One

Stories of Faith, Family and Community

I loved to be around my elderly family members when they talked and interacted with each other. It was deliberate, loving, sharing, informative and above all, soothing. They pondered life, solved problems and worked together to ensure family and community survival.

While spending time at home with my parents, I would take my mother to visit her "sister-friends" in the neighborhood and those who had moved out as well. Even though I was an adult, I still remembered to be quiet and respectful while "grown folks" were talking, lessons that stayed with me from my childhood growing up among those same women and men. I was mesmerized as I sat listening to the elders talk. Their stories recounted a time that I never knew or one that I vaguely remembered from my own childhood. I looked forward to the visits and to the stories with great anticipation. I knew that I would learn something new about these people who were so important in my life.

I now know that these were the **griots**, the men and women who kept the stories for my family and community. When I had my son, I would take him along to be around the storytellers and to hear their tales. He was a special gift to the elders, especially the women. His presence triggered stories of their young motherhood, of child care arrangements, of balancing farm work and raising children, and of how different children are now than they use to be. "They are getting weaker and wiser, now that's bible," the women always lamented.

The opportunity to sit with these elders, around their kitchen tables or around their wood heaters, and to listen to their stories no longer exists for me. Many of the elders have died or moved away or time has stolen their sense of the distant and recent past along with its stories. Since those special times have passed, I had to devise a way to recapture those stories, to share them, and to be renewed and invigorated by them. I had to write them myself and share them with an audience which could benefit from hearing or reading about the lives of those elders who helped to shape their corner of the world.

I encourage everyone to record and tell stories, not just because it is fulfilling, interesting and is a tribute to family, but also because it is a valuable way to preserve culture. Stories help us to have a better knowledge and understanding of ourselves; they help us to become aware of who we are as a group and where we belong. Telling stories is a way to empower people, to unshroud the lives of our ancestors, and to illuminate strengths and problem-solving strategies while providing viable options and instilling a communal spirit. Stories can bond the old and the young, the living and those who have transitioned.

I hope this collection of stories and profiles of elders will encourage you to speak of stories and to see the imperative of safeguarding legacies and memories through stories. I consider this business of collecting and sharing African American stories sacred and soul-quieting work that nourishes the heart and mind. Join me.

*Ph*lox in Early Spring

After much discussion the Crosspoint Home Demonstration Club finally found a community beautification project they could all agree on. They decided to plant flowers in the fork in the road by the mailbox where the dirt roads intersected forming a near perfect triangular section of land. A flower garden, they all agreed, would be a considerable improvement, as the plot of ground in question had always been covered with weeds and worrisome sand spurs for as long as anyone could remember.

One day early in the spring, the club members, Mama and the other women in the neighborhood, all met at the triangle in the road with a determined spirit, their freshly sharpened hoes, and lots of packs of flower seeds to complete their beautification project. They chopped the triangle mound clean, turning the soil over just so, and then planted pink, white and violet **phlox** seeds.

The flowers bloomed beautifully that spring and every spring thereafter covering the triangle garden like a colorful blanket. In the bright sun and the well-drained sandy soil of southeastern North Carolina, the phlox thrived.

Today, some forty years later, the phlox continue to bloom each spring. But, there are very few of the flowers still on the original triangle mound. Thanks to the birds, the wind, the rain and the state road maintenance crews, the seeds have spread and the phlox now bloom all along the sides of the road, into the edge of the fields and down into the ditches. It's as if the flowers are determined travelers spreading to each of the five club women's homes and blanketing the community in their memory.

I wonder if the women ever imagined that the delicate candy-colored flowers would outlive them.

*W*hen the Home Demonstration
Club Agent Didn't Come

Miss Anita Johnson was elegant, stately, well-spoken, attractive, educated and humble. The women of Carltontown really respected, admired and were awed by Miss Johnson. They welcomed her into their midst once per month like a routine doctor's visit. She was the Home Demonstration Club agent from the Agricultural Extension Office, and the Home Demonstration Club that she supervised was an important educational component of these farm women's lives. Each month the club would meet at a different member's house and the agent would "demonstrate" some modern, new or better way to maintain or enhance the home. It could have been canning fruit or arranging flowers. Whatever the demonstration, the women all testified that they learned a lot. Yet they also all admitted that they had the most fun at the meetings when the agent had come and gone.

The club meetings were held during the weekday in the early afternoon. The hostess cleaned her house thoroughly and prepared a special meal for the members. Mama always made us polish the furniture especially the dinning room set which had far to many grooves for my fingers and the Ole English furniture polish rag. The process took hours.

Mama, like each of the women who hosted the meeting, made some delectable dishes that we did not usually have. The menu always included ambrosia and deep-dish apple pie, and a few other delicacies. We loved club day and could hardly wait for school to end so we could get home and feast on the leftovers.

After the business meeting and the demonstration, the meal was served. The whole occasion was special because it gave the Carltontown women a chance to stop farming, to dress up and to spend time with each other. But it wasn't leisure. It was purposeful. They had no understanding of leisure. Time was too precious, and there was far too much to do.

The women were on their best behavior while the agent was there. They were careful that their subjects agreed with their verbs. They tried to act proper, to ask intelligent questions and to always maintain their decorum. They were very relieved when Miss Johnson left so they could be themselves again, a little less proper. That's when they really began to have fun. They laughed and joked with each other and laughed at each other's stories about their husbands. They were attentive to each other's needs. They comforted each other. They offered advice, but mostly they just spent good and valuable time with each other.

The Home Demonstration Clubs were segregated because the White women about a quarter of a mile up the road had their own club and they had a White agent to demonstrate in their homes. I always wondered if they tried to sound and act intelligent for their agent and if they had as much fun as Mama and her sister friends had after their agent left.

The Easter Egg Hunt

"Allieeeee" is the call that wafted across the corn field to Aunt Allie Bethel's house. They didn't use the telephone for things like this. The telephone was for business and the call to Aunt Allie was for pleasure. It was time for the annual neighborhood Easter Egg Hunt. This hunt had become a tradition in Crosspoint. It took place either Sunday afternoon after church or Easter Monday. . . usually Sunday because Monday was a work day on the farm. On the occasion of the last Easter Egg Hunt that I remember, the children, at least in my generation, were grown, home on holiday to visit family, and their children were the ones who would pursue the eggs.

We met at the fork in the road and hid the eggs in the dry brown grass. There had not been enough warm days for the pale green sprigs of spring to begin breaking through the hard dry earth. The elder women, like Mama and Aunt Allie, were the traditional leaders of the hiding brigade. Like soldiers on a mission, they took their job seriously and tried to remember where each egg was placed. The next generation, my sister, brother, cousins and I had to help our children to find the eggs—a sign that we hadn't quite arrived into real adulthood. We certainly weren't the "elders." Secretly, we relished the idea that this gave us the chance to hunt too. We weren't ready to give up on that part of the childhood tradition. It felt too good. It was a time when the women in the community embraced us all like warm quilts, and we felt safe and secure. We were a little ambivalent about giving up our place, but we wanted our children to have those same feelings and emotions that comforted us.

On this day, Aunt Allie was late, but we knew that she was coming and nothing started until she got there. Aunt Allie had her own unique way of doing things and of thinking about life. For example, she always referred to some of her sisters and brothers as Sis Maggie, or Sis Bertha or Bud Willie or Bud Jo. Once I asked her why she put these handles on some of her sisters and brothers' names and not on others. She explained that those were the older ones of her siblings and that it would be disrespectful to call them by their first names. Even though they were her sisters and brothers, they were still grown.

 As we all stood around in the road waiting for Aunt Allie, the children started to get a little impatient. In the blink of an eye, Aunt Allie came running out of her front door heading down the road toward us. Of course, she had her eggs to contribute to the ones that the other households had brought. Aunt Allie didn't have children or grandchildren at the egg hunt, but that certainly didn't prevent her eager participation. And we wouldn't have had the egg hunt without her. She completed the community circle.

Aunt Allie was the person whom children loved. She spoke their language and gave them endless hours of fun with her easy humor. Her laugh was all of a sudden and surprising like a clap of thunder. She could make you feel like everyday was Sunday afternoon after church. Each of the brown eggs that Aunt Allie brought that day had three to five scribbled lines of bright colored crayon on them. She explained that she was late because she had to *color* her eggs. So the hiding began with Aunt Allie's brown bespeckled eggs joining the others tucked between the dry brown grass with the pale green sprigs of spring struggling for light and life.

We Loved and Feared the Tin Roof

We always had a tin roof on our house. We loved that roof when it rained. The pitter patter of the rain falling on that roof could lull you into a deep peaceful sleep, the kind of sleep you enjoyed when Mama gently spread a second quilt over you late on a winter night.

But Mama never liked that tin roof. When the thunderstorm came across the field from Cousin Lillie Bell's house, Mama gathered my sister, brother and me in the living room. She said to be quiet, "The Lord is doing His work." She was always scared when the summer thunderstorms came, but hurricane season really terrified her. We lived in hurricane ally, 50 miles from the ocean. We never went to the ocean except when the Sunday School took their annual trip to the Black section of Topsail Beach because the Atlantic Ocean was segregated when I was growing up. So, if a hurricane came ashore in North Carolina, we were sure to get it and sure to be frightened because we were never prepared for the deadly combination of wind and water. Mama was always scared that the wind would get under the edge of the ole roll-tin and blow the roof off of the house. We never really understood why Mama was so concerned because the roof made it through lots of storms including Hurricane Hazel—the big category four hurricane of 1954.

Even after we grew up and moved away, we secretly and sometimes openly wished for a good rainstorm when we came home for a visit so we could sleep under the tin roof with peaceful, soothing rain falling. Daddy could read the clouds, and I'm sure if we lived on the ocean, he would have been able to read the waves too. So when we came home, we asked Daddy if it was gonna rain that day. He had a better success rate than the weather man on television. Daddy would look up, squint his eyes, rub his balding head and thoughtfully respond. "Not tonight, the clouds are breaking up" or "I 'spect we'll get a little rain over in the night, but it won't do no good because it'll be salt water. It's coming off the ocean." I always thought water was water, and it never occurred to me that rain water from the east was from the Atlantic Ocean, salty and not very beneficial to the crops.

In 1997, Hurricane Fran found its way under the edge of the tin, rolled it up, and off it blew across the road and into Cousin Oliver's field. The tin lay there in the field and road crushed and discarded like old farm equipment on land long abandoned by its owners. Hurricane Fran poured rain in the house for hours destroying the house and the furniture. Mama wasn't there. Daddy had transitioned the year before.

Mama was right about the wind and the Lord's work and that ole tin roof even though it lasted fifty years before the wind got under the corners and hurled it around, finally bringing it to rest in the field across the road.

*G*loria & James

Gloria and James were high school sweethearts. They married young. Some say it was because Gloria's mother died when she was so young, and motherless children are prone to search for love. Both Gloria and James helped us **barn tobacco**.

Thursday was our day to **put-in tobacco**. Everybody in the neighborhood had different days for bringing in the cash crop so they could help each other. Daddy had gone to pick up the help. We had been up since 4:00 that morning because we had to take the dry tobacco out of the barn while the dew was out so we could then put the green tobacco in.

By the time Daddy got back, we had finished breakfast and were on our way to the tobacco barn. Gloria and James took up their stations of work, James in the field with the other men cropping the green leaf, and Gloria at the tobacco barn with the women and girls, "handing" and "looping" the fist-sized, dew-drenched bundles.

Gloria was particularly sad that day. She looked like the slightest jar would send tears spilling from her eyes. Her mood was heavy like sad news and darkness, and all the women at the barn, especially the elders like, Mama and Cousin Bee, seemed to feel her pain.

As the morning wore on, I saw each of the elder women one-by-one approach Gloria out of earshot from the rest of us. They spoke to her in hushed tones. They were gentle making no effort to cheer her just to comfort and teach her.

After each encounter Gloria's spirits began to change and lift like clouds burning away on an overcast morning.

I asked Mama later that night what they were saying to Gloria. "We just told her, 'child don't wear your heart on your sleeves,'" Mama said softly. I never found out what trouble had come to Gloria and sapped her spirit so, but I do know that on that day Gloria got wonderful gifts of love and wisdom from caring and giving elder women, gifts that she tucked away for safe keeping until life's circumstances necessitated their retrieval at some later date.

*G*etting Out The Vote

That second Tuesday in November 1984, Uncle Theodore stopped by the house on his way home from the polls. I asked him who he voted for president. Beaming with a sly sparkle in his eyes, he straightened his 88-year old six-feet three inch frame, rocked back a little on his heels like a new CEO, and said, "You know I voted for Jesse Jackson. I'm so glad that I had the opportunity to vote for a Black man for president one time in life before I died." I was a little surprised that he felt so strongly. I had never heard him or many of the other folk in Crosspoint talk a lot about race pride although they talked a lot about family pride. Maybe it was one in the same. And I was also a little surprised that voting for a Black person would mean so much to him, even though it meant a lot to me.

Voting . . . the activity and process, was a ritual in Crosspoint. Watching the World Series and voting were two of the most serious activities that Mama and Daddy engaged in together—and enjoyed. They were Democrats, but not the **yellow dog** type. They always felt the need to vote for the best person running regardless of the party. The party, however, was usually democratic.

Many times the people in the neighborhood would meet at our house on Election Day, caucus, and go to the poles together. They voted in a block. Because Daddy was the only one among them engaged in **public work**, they reckoned that he might have a little more insight. They listened to him about these matters and took their right to vote very seriously. When the neighbors didn't ride together in the same car, couples made the trip together. I always felt some sense of pride when my family (extended and fictive) drove by our house on their way to and from the polls.

The vote was a big deal and my folks took that right and responsibility seriously. The trip to the polls was as important as fourth Sunday church service—sacred and not to be missed.

*T*here Are People Who
Need It Worse Than Me

On Wednesday morning before Thanksgiving I asked Daddy to go with me down to Holtsville to apply for the Low-Income Energy Assistance program. "It's a little money to help you and Mama to pay for the gas to heat the house this winter," I told them. Daddy said, "I don't have time" or some such weak excuse. I asked again. After several attempts, he would say, "They ain't gonna give me nothing." I said "maybe not, but lets try." He finally said okay.

I always tried to tell the folks about social service benefits that might be available to them. They weren't eligible for most programs because they were landowners. They loved their land and were always scared that it might get taken from them somehow—a practice they had witnessed many times when Whites decided they wanted a Black family's land. They saw any kind of farm loan as a threat to their land and were reluctant to apply for the few loans that were actually available to Black farmers.

Daddy and his brothers were very proud to be landowners. Whenever the opportunity presented itself, they always tried to buy " a little piece of land" here or there. The most recent piece of land acquired was always called "the new ground." "The new ground" could have been bought 30 years earlier, but if it was the most recent purchase, it was "the new ground." The saying among my folks was "they ain't making no more land." The land was precious and was NEVER to be sold outside the family.

Getting handouts from the government was always a threat to the land. My folks were paranoid and it had helped them to stay safe and to keep what they worked for. So when Daddy said okay, he'd apply for the fuel subsidy, I was shocked and hurriedly said "let's go" before he could change his mind.

I drove him to the office in Holtsville. As we approached the nondescript corrugated building, Daddy seemed to sense static in the air like right before a storm, but he persevered. We went through a relatively painless process that did not embarrass or belittle him. He was eligible for the one-time fuel subsidy which was scheduled to get to him sometime the following February.

Daddy was encouraged by the process and felt like applying for something else. So he said, "I'd like to apply for food stamps." I was shocked again and hurried Daddy over to the other office so he could apply for the food stamps. Again, he was eligible like I knew he would be. He and Mama were eligible for the minimal per month allotment . . . about $12. It was still a victory. I finally got Daddy to apply for some social service benefits even though there were others who needed them worse than he did. When the $78 came for the fuel, they paid the gas bill; it helped a lot.

Daddy and Mama never used the food stamps though. The food stamps arrived each month and Mama and Daddy "put them away" as if to accrue interest. My sister and I would go over to do their monthly grocery shopping and ask where they had put the food stamps.

"Look over there on the desk or maybe your Daddy (or maybe your Mother) put them on the dresser" was their response.

 My sister and I would track them down and add that $12 to the money for the groceries. But Mama and Daddy never acknowledged the food stamps. They never used them and didn't seem to care whether they came in the mail or not because they intended to promptly put them away to accumulate like dust balls under the edge of the bed until the next month's food stamps arrived or until my sister and I found them and did their monthly grocery shopping.

*H*ome from the Hospital

With a look of fear, but an air of acceptance and resolve, Mama asked if I thought that the doctors had "given up" on Daddy to send him home in his condition. Surely in her mind, they must have given up on him. Mama was worried because Daddy had been discharged from the hospital with a **Foley catheter**. Having something foreign attached to the body like that really confused our parents. Daddy was clear that he was sick and that the sick role was the right one to take. But when the home health nurse tied the bag to Daddy's leg and disconnected him from the IV pole, he was not sure if he should take on the sick role or the well role. He decided to be "well" and set off to "farm" and to feed the hogs.

The home health team added further confusion to the situation. The registered nurse came out to the house to do the initial paper work and to explain about home health. The nursing assistant came regularly, about three times a week. She came to help Daddy with his bath, to clean his sitting and sleeping areas, to prepare light meals and to do his laundry.

Daddy was usually a good patient and was very comfortable with the nurse and the nursing assistant, but not Mama. Mama would get up early each morning when the nursing assistant was scheduled to come. She'd help Daddy bathe, change into clean pajamas, change his bed linen, have the wash going and the breakfast cooking. Focused and meticulous, she was like a new bride preparing for her mother-in-law's first visit.

We constantly begged Mama to let the nurse and nursing assistants do their jobs and reminded her that she was doing everything and there was nothing left for them to do. Like a worker bee, Mama had lived all of her life with no one except her children ever doing any housework or cooking for her. She was not able to understand the nursing assistant's role. To Mama, the nursing assistant was a stranger who visited several times per week. She was a guest.

Finally, when I tried again to understand Mama's behavior and to ask her to please stop cleaning up for the nursing assistant, she responded with the wounded innocence of a confused child, "You can't have people coming into your home with it looking any kinda way," she declared.

The nursing assistant arrived one morning to find Daddy outside, his 80 year old frame weakly weaving to the pack house to get feed to take to the animals. She recognized his frail state and tried to help. He insisted that the feed buckets were too heavy for her, and he would take care of it. She accompanied him to feed the animals because she knew that he might, in his weakened state, fall or be knocked down by the animals. After they returned to the house, the nursing assistant finally accepted one of Mama's many invitations to join them for a meal. From then on the nursing assistant could do no wrong. They looked forward to her "visits." She was still a visitor, a guest, but one who could be trusted. They decided to "let" her help them.

The Blueberry Bus

Daddy hated to see me get on that blueberry bus. The blueberry bus wasn't even blue, but it carried day laborers to the blueberry field. A seasonal regular, the bus arrived every morning at 6:30 like summer sunshine. The bus took me and Aunt Cullie to the blueberry fields somewhere about twenty miles away down Highway 11.

Daddy hated for me to get on the bus because he said that there was enough work for me to do at home on the farm. Secretly, I believe Daddy hated for any of us, especially me and my sister—the girls—to do any work away from the farm for other people because he would lose control and most importantly, he would lose his ability to protect us from racial slurs and disrespect when we were out in the world.

But, I loved picking blueberries. I was so good at it. I could roll the berries off into my hand, drop them into the cup tied around my waist and never miss a beat. We were paid by the amount picked, so I earned enough to help with my school clothes and books.

My blueberry picking days never embarrassed me. Lots of high school and college kids did it. But thoughts of riding the blueberry bus still embarrass me a little. I don't really know why. Maybe it symbolizes a loss of innocence, knowing that there would come a time when Daddy and my extended family couldn't protect me from a world that could be cruel and exploitive to people like us.

$\mathcal{D}$riving

Mama was always a good and careful driver. But she never seemed to enjoy driving; it was like so many other things in her life—necessary. She recalled one Sunday on her way home from church when she got to the "t" intersection at Mr. Bep Turner's house she became really "confused." She didn't know if she should turn or keep straight. So she just stopped. This was a drive that she had made for over 50 years. What really scared her was that she realized that she was beginning to lose her memory. She never drove to church again.

Driving had meant freedom, and it kept people connected. Not being able to drive meant dependence and sometimes isolation for rural people. Even after Mama decided not to drive anymore, she still got her license renewed. On September 25, 1980, five days before her 67th birthday, when Mama successfully renewed her license for the last time, she beamed with the excitement and pride of a schoolgirl winning a special prize. But she knew that she wasn't ever going to risk the confusion and fear that she felt that

Sunday at the intersection coming home from church. So she never used her brand new driver's license.

Singing in the Choir on Sunday Morning

Marching into the church in their royal blue robes with the gold satin collars made the Second Baptist Church Senior Choir appear especially majestic. All of the women had a confident swagger accentuated by the swinging of their Sunday pocketbooks. Most of the choir members were elderly and their best singing days were behind them. But the Sunday morning air, the promenade, Mr. Harry's piano music, and the chance to praise the Lord, fueled their spirits and raised their voices in song.

Mama sang in the church choir nearly every Fourth Sunday. We had church service once a month—on the fourth Sunday. Mama had a nice rich alto voice. She led songs some Sundays. My sister and I watched with our fingers crossed hoping that she wouldn't "**get happy**" and embarrass us with too much show of emotion. Some Sundays she did and we tried our best to become invisible to our peers who sat with us.

One Sunday, Miss Fannie, an ample lady who always sat in the first seat on the front row, remarked that she knew that Mama was there because she always smelled her Listerine. Mama had relied on the Listerine to rid her mouth of the smell and taste of snuff; but Miss Fannie's remark really embarrassed her so Mama decided to try another mouthwash, one that would not announce her coming before she arrived.

Mama knew that she had a pretty voice, and she liked it, but sometimes it made her sad.

She didn't sing very much at home, but when she did, we knew that there was something heavy on her heart.

It made us feel especially helpless. But Mama used singing as therapy, as an escape, a way to work through her problems. Once she had dealt with the problem or come to some resolution, she stopped singing and her spirits lifted like the brightness that streaked through the window when the shades are raised early on a summer morning.

*C*astor Oil on Saturday Morning

It was as if the ledge around the wood heater was made to hold the bottle of castor oil. The flat bottle hugged the heater and warmed slowly early one Saturday morning as the weather was turning cold. It didn't heat to boiling; just enough to glide easily down our throats like slimy steamed okra.

Taking castor oil was a late fall, early winter ritual in our house. Each of the three youngest kids had to line up for our annual dose of the nasty, dreaded elixir.

My oldest brother—20 years my senior—made it a practice to come out on Saturday mornings to help with the ritual. It was all done to fortify us against the threat of winter cold and flu, protecting our bodies like that thick plastic that covers the windows of houses in the wintertime to keep the wind and cold out.

We had to be brave because there was no way to avoid it. Seeing our parents reach into the far corner of the kitchen cabinet for castor oil spelled impending doom. Mama had the oranges cut in half to chase the oil and to help it to stay *down*. She had the largest tablespoon in the world, and we lined up when she gave the order. My oldest brother would hold us down because regardless of how brave we planned to be, the sight of the oil on the heater's ledge turned our nerves to mush and seemed to put wings on our feet.

After Mama put the tablespoon of oil in our mouths, she'd hurriedly squeeze the orange half so that the juice was dripping by the time it got to our mouths. Mama repeated in a coaxing but firm voice, "swallow it down, swallow it down."

We were all lucky that this only happened once per year. We still got winter colds, sometimes got the flu and always got tonsillitis. But maybe it would have been much worse without the castor oil. It was certainly a risk that we were willing to take. The Saturday morning castor oil ritual is one that didn't carry over to our own children.

$\boldsymbol{O}$e Lady Ngo

Her name was Dr. Corazino Ngo, but Daddy took an impish delight in calling his doctor "Ole Lady Ngo." I think it was out of some combination of affection and respect. It had a rhythmic sound like just the right blend of voices in the Sunday choir and Daddy liked to hear himself say it. The doctor had a rural practice filled with elderly folks. Whenever Daddy became ill, we had to almost force him to go to the doctor. He would reason that he really couldn't go because he still owed her from the last visit and should wait until he paid her all that was owed before he returned.

After some coaxing, Daddy and I arrived at the doctor's office one day when he wasn't feel well. Daddy put his Pall Mall cigarette out flicking the fire off the end and being careful not to crush the long butt that was left. After he was sure the fire was gone, he started to put the butt in his shirt pocket but changed his mind and placed it in the car ashtray instead. He responded to my puzzled look by saying that he didn't want "Ole lady Ngo" to see the cigarette and he didn't want to "hear her mouth."

Daddy was comfortable with the patient role. Mama always accused him of pretending to be sick whenever we came home for visits so that he could get our attention and be coddled. That could have been true, or maybe he held on to his health until we came and then he gave his body permission to collapse since he had someone to take him to the doctor.

Whatever the truth, whenever I took him to see "Ole lady Ngo," she always treated a *real*—not imagined—ailment.

$\mathcal{H}$ospital Psychosis

Daddy was admitted to the hospital early in the spring. His blood was very low and he was extremely weak. The first time this happened, Daddy was in his late 70s. He became very confused in the hospital, and he began to hallucinate. My sister and I were terrified. We had never seen Daddy like this before. His personality had changed completely. The nurses asked us if he was usually this way.

When we got a chance to talk with the doctor, himself an elderly man, we asked him if our father had suffered some type of brain damage that was causing the confusion and hallucination. The doctor matter-of-factly responded "Oh no, he's just an old man in the hospital."

I thought that his response was not a very reasonable explanation, and I wanted to say . . . "you are an old man in the hospital, and you're not hallucinating."

My sister and I could have been saved a lot of hours of anguish if someone had done a better job explaining to us that elders in hospitals can sometimes get confused because of the new environment, the change in routine, the poking and prodding of the medical personnel throughout the day and night and the illness or injury itself which landed them in the hospital in the first place.

My sister and I weren't so afraid the next few times that Daddy went into the hospital and began to hallucinate. We were even able to see some humor in his new and more exuberant personality. Even though we could now give the behavior a name—hospital psychosis—we were still fearful that Daddy might not come back to himself.

An even more dreadful aspect of this hospitalization was that he was restrained both medically and physically. The doctor put him on Haldol. It wasn't good. We insisted that the doctors take him off of it because of the side effects. The doctor was not impressed with us and was affronted that we would make such a request of him—the expert. He wanted to know "what we did for a living" and where we worked. I simply wanted him to use a less harsh drug. I'm still wondering what our inquiries about our Daddy's health care had to do with our career choices and places of employment.

*W*hen Miss Theene Died

Miss Theene was Cousin Julia's mother. To us children she was always old. She couldn't see, and she always sat quietly in the same chair in Cousin Julia's living room. Cousin Julia had brothers and sisters, but for some reason, she took care of Miss Theene, and the others just visited once or twice a year. I never heard Cousin Julia complain about having to take responsibility for Miss Theene alone though. She just took care of her mother and welcomed her brothers and sisters when they visited.

The children in the neighborhood were really surprised when Miss Theene died. We just thought she never would.

Everybody in the neighborhood went to Cousin Julia's house to see if they could do anything to help. A steady stream of visitors came and went all day.

Cousin Julia decided to bring Miss Theene's body home for the "**settin-up**," so the room had to be readied. All of the furniture was taken out and a thick red velvet curtain was hung against one wall. The mirrors were covered to make sure that Miss Theene's spirit wouldn't be trapped in the room.

The coffin carrying Miss Theene was parked in front of the velvet curtain where it stayed all night. Torch lamp lights stood at each end of the coffin like stately sentries at their guard post. Family stayed up with Miss Theene throughout the night as well. They ate, talked, drank, laughed, reminisced and moaned Miss Theene's death.

After the funeral and burial, the room was returned to its usual order. Miss Theene's chair stayed in the same place for a long time though and nobody ever sat in it. The children thought Miss Theene was still in the chair; we couldn't see her, but we were sure the grown folks did.

$\mathcal{T}$he Ole Wood Heater

Mama had light almost white spots on her dark brown legs just in the front. We believed that the spots came from sitting too close to the heater when it was real hot. Each morning during the winter Mama got up first to make the fire in the wood stove. Unless the winter night was really cold the wood stove heated two, almost three, of the six rooms in the house.

Mama remembered the time when she also had to cook on a wood stove. I don't.

When someone came into the house on a very cold day they would go to the heater and warm themselves with their hands extended as if to beckon the heat toward them.

All of the houses in the neighborhood had wood stoves for heat. The houses' poor construction with no underpinning, no insulation, and no storm windows and doors did little to discourage the cold. Whenever you'd go to someone's house they would greet you with a "come on in and pull up a chair" meaning pull the chair up closer to the heater. They would sometimes offer food, (especially if they were eating) but would always offer to share heat from the ole wood stove.

The heater was a central part of all the homes. In winter you could always find families sitting near the fire. That's what the heaters were called. Uncle Henry would lie on the floor in front of his heater. Cousin Janie had her chair and company chairs strategically placed in a semi circle around the heater. To preserve the heat most folks used the room with the heater for most activities. For some, the heater was in a bedroom. Uncle Henry's heater was in the den/dining room. Uncle Bryant's was in his setting room. Our heater was in Mama and Daddy's bedroom. Wherever the heater was was where people gathered, and it was the room that guests went to when they visited.

The heat was the welcome mat and the warmth stimulated discussions of weather forecasts and ultimately planting season. My folks didn't waste words though. They never said "the cold weather," just "The Cold" like it was some powerful well-known entity familiar enough to be known by one name sorta like Hitler, Roosevelt, or Cher. "Pull up a chair" was an invitation to make oneself comfortable . . . sitting or standing. My cousin Boot never sat down, but was always invited to "pull up a chair and to come on in out of the Cold."

In recent years when I read in the newspapers, usually the Lifestyle Section, about the art of making a fire, I feel a little sad for people who don't know how to make a fire. Everybody in my neighborhood knew how to make a fire, how to cut wood, how to place kindling, which we called "light wood," so that it got the fire started, and how to stoke the fire or as we said "tend" the fire to keep it going.

The old wood heater had a central place in our home and in our neighbors' homes. The well-worn area around the heater attested to family time spent engaged in staying warm, visiting, parching peanuts, doing homework . . . making do, and being together.

*W*hen Aunt Cullie
Started to Wander

It was about 1:00 in the morning. It was late fall and starting to get cool outside. Mama and Daddy were asleep when someone knocked on the back door. People didn't stop by that time of morning unless something real bad had happened. Giving each other that "wonder-who-that-could-be-look," Mama and Daddy both got up together to answer the door.

It was Aunt Cullie. She had a still, blank look in her eyes and she was trying to find her daughter Bonita. But Bonita no longer lived in our neighborhood. She had been living in New York for over 35 years. Aunt Cullie said that she heard Bonita call for her, and she believed that her daughter was there.

It was a scary time, because we knew that Aunt Cullie was changing. When Mama called Aunt Cullie's husband, Uncle Bryant to tell him that she was up at our house, he was alarmed and surprised because he hadn't heard her leave their house. He came up to get her to take her back home. He said that he had seen some changes in her lately, but this wandering, he knew, was very dangerous. He paused, shaking his head and looking downward, as if searching to find some answers in the cold faded linoleum on the kitchen floor.

That next week, Aunt Cullie made another early morning visit to her niece's house further up the road. Aunt Cullie was still looking for her only child Bonita.

Uncle Bryant telephoned Bonita.

About a month later, Bonita came home from New York and moved Aunt Cullie away. The following summer Bonita brought Aunt Cullie home for a visit. We all walked down the road to see her. She looked good; her skin was beautiful and flawless. She seemed more like her old self, but we were told that her mind would come and go. That was the last time we saw our aunt.

We knew that Aunt Cullie was leaving our neighborhood for good, but that reality was too burdensome, so we smiled anyway and waved good-bye as we watched Bonita's station wagon head up the road taking Aunt Cullie to live out her days far away from Carltontown in New York.

$\mathcal{T}$he Night the
Barn Burned Down

It was about 2:00 in the morning, and everyone was asleep. My sister who was home for a visit had turned in early, but the lowing of the cows woke her from a sound sleep. As she opened her eyes, she saw the bedroom covered in a bright reflection coming from the tin-covered shelter. She ran to the door and saw flames shooting high into the sky at the end of the field. The tobacco barn was burning. She woke Mama and Daddy, who though startled and arthritic, struggled to respond to the emergency. Daddy's eyes rolled back in his head and his body went limp like a rain-drenched person who has resigned himself to being soaked. He seemed about to faint. Everyone worked to stabilize him.

This wasn't the first time that this fiery tragedy struck my parents' farm. I was a little girl when the barn burned the first time. I don't remember the fire itself, but images of my aunts, uncles, and cousins' urgent responses are still vivid. I remember Cousin Argie crying as she ran with buckets of water. The family almost instinctively formed a human chain passing buckets of water from one to the other working their way down to the burning barn. While their efforts seemed futile, nobody dared quit. This time instead of relying on family to douse the flames, my sister called the fire department. The biggest fear was that the fire would cause the fuel tank to explode spreading the fire to the house and nearby woods. In minutes the whole scene became mass confusion. The firemen didn't know how to get to my parents' house. My sister tried to give them directions as the rest of us watched helplessly while the barn burned. Exasperated, she finally called our oldest brother who guided the volunteer fire fighters out to the farm.

They put the fire out. The barn and all of its contents were destroyed. When the water hit the fuel tank, it sizzled like bacon in a hot frying pan.

On the radio the next morning, the announcer said in a detached, matter-of-fact monotone that silenced all of us at the breakfast table, "Fire truck went to Willie Elwood's place on State Road 1173 this morning around 2:00 . . . tobacco barn fire."

Daddy was quieter than usual for the next few days. Sometime during the fire, he had decided he would not grow tobacco another year. Two flames went out that dewy summer morning, the tobacco barn fire and the one in our Daddy's eyes. For him, a way of life was coming to an end.

$\mathcal{H}$og Killing Day

Mama and all of the other women wore layers of thick old clothing to protect them from the 25 degree February day. They busied themselves carrying pots, pans, bowls, spices, detergent, cleavers and such out of the house to the two long makeshift tables set up in the yard. It was hog killing day. All of the neighbors had come to help with the day-long ritual.

The preparation started well before the designated day. Mr. Murfree had brought the big black pot over. I was never quite sure who owned the pot. It just seemed to appear, moving from house to house as needed. Wood had been cut and placed round the pot. Daddy had spent the previous day "settin'-up," sharpening the knives and cleavers, digging the hole over which the vat was placed, and attaching the cast-iron meat grinder to the table in the yard.

Mama made sure that all of the spices were on hand. Rubbing sage seemed to have been the master spice of that day.

The hogs had been identified and isolated a few days before and the men made their way to the pen. The hogs were shot between the eyes, a quick death to keep fear out of the meat, and then put in a vat of boiling water to ease the removal of hair.

As family members aged, handling the rifle became an especially tricky prospect. On one occasion, tragedy struck, albeit not fatally, when Mr. A.J. shot Uncle Benjamin as he aimed for the skittish hog. This created an emergency run to the hospital. On this day, however, the hogs were the only ones shot. It was the custom to kill two or three hogs at a time.

The ritual progressed with family working against the short day of winter to get the job done. There were so many different parts to this hog killing ordeal. The women had special roles and so did the men. Children didn't usually experience hog killings because they took place on school days. But, my older brother remembers that his childhood job on hog killing day was to keep the fire burning hot under the big black pot.

The pot used to cook the fat to make the lard had been placed in the center of activity in the yard. Daddy, who was a professional meat cutter, had the responsibility of cutting the animals up. That was the job reserved for his skills at everyone's hog killing as well.

Cousin Julia made especially delicious sausage adding just the right blend of spices to the meat. Others had their specialties too. I remember the skill and ease with which the women stuffed the moist casings with sausage and pudding securing the ends by tying them off with a string. Stuffing the casings was a fast paced job and the women guided the filled casing with relative ease forming various links of the breakfast staples.

All day long the chilly air was filled with meticulous cutting, slicing and scrapping along with light-hearted conversation, storytelling and lots of laughter. The laughter seemed to cut the subfreezing chill, warming things up like the smell of roasted peanuts just out of a hot oven. A big dinner was prepared for the hog killing workers. Dinner always included some of "**the fresh**," their term for the hog meat from that day's kill—meat that had not been cured.

The kitchen was always a mess on hog killing day and it was always cold in the house due to constant traffic in and out throughout the day.

As the day's labor drew to an end, the women began to bring in the knives and cleavers they had worked with all day. And the pots and pans they balanced on their hips were filled with rings of sausage and pudding that was sure to spice up breakfast for many months to come. Cleaning the outside work area meant bringing everything indoors thus overrunning the kitchen with smells and greasy cutlery.

When everyone went home, Mama and Daddy had to complete the work. Mama wrapped the meat, sausage, and pudding, carefully labeled it, and put it in the freezer. She stored the **cracklins** which were the last products from the black pot. Within days she would make **souse** meat, and clean and soak the chitterlings again before adding them to the overstocked deep freezer.

Daddy smoked and salted down the larger pieces of meat like the shoulders and the hams, eventually sold some and kept the others to feed the family until another cold winter day a year later when the supply could be replenished with another hog killing.

Few items from the hogs were wasted. I vividly remember the hog brains in the bowl in the refrigerator. I believe Mama scrambled them with eggs for breakfast. Some considered this dish a delicacy. I'm not among them.

I often remember hog killing day with its flurry of activity, but it was one of my least favorite activities. If I never see another bowl of brains in the refrigerator, it will be too soon. Eventually hog killing day, which actually dragged on for several days, was over when there was nothing left to look at and nothing left to smell.

Yet the spirit of family and community that prevails on that day continues to resonate with me. Hog killings like barn raisings and quilting bees were part of the ritual of survival for people in my community.

$\mathcal{P}$art Two

Profiles of Elderly African American Farm Women

Historically, no struggle for social justice and institutional transformation has ever developed without a concomitant struggle for group survival. Elderly African American farm women have been central to the struggle for group social change as well as survival and uplift within the rural African American farm community. Social workers, historians, and other scholars and researchers have long neglected the value and impact of the African American farm woman's role and function in this historically significant effort. The result is that we know little about the importance and value of their function as workers, wives, mothers and community leaders. Our lack of knowledge leads us to minimize their contributions and general worth to society.

The African American farm population has declined at a rate much faster than that of the White farm population. In 1980, one percent of African Americans and three percent of Whites lived on farms. With jobs outside the farm becoming more accessible and with the rate of "Black land loss" and out-migration increasing, African American farm women in North Carolina are rapidly declining as a group. Elderly African American farm women (ages 65 and older), however, continue to live on and work the land that they have inhabited for 50 years or more. They have seen numerous transitions in their lives, and the lives of their neighbors. These women have not stood by quietly and watched their communities change, rather they have been a major force in shaping and protecting their communities.

These women have formally and informally adopted children or simply taken needy children into their homes whenever the circumstances warranted. Their children were taught the value of work and were gainfully (unless ill) employed in skilled trades and/or professions. Some have their own businesses. All of these women valued formal education and, with few exceptions, have provided the encouragement, moral and financial support to see their children graduate from some of the most reputable colleges and universities throughout the country. Many of their children hold terminal degrees in their fields. The women take great pride in their children's accomplishments and modestly take none of the credit.

Through the use of verbatim statements taken from the interviews with ten elderly farm women in southeastern North Carolina, this section illuminates a dimension of African American history and culture that, given current trends, may be lost in our near future. Through open-ended questions, I asked each woman about her life as a farm woman, her experiences during the Great Depression years, her wedding day, her needs, and the things that have given her the most pleasure and joy in life. Their responses are an important contribution without my professional commentary and are presented with little interpretation. These women were quite capable of speaking for themselves and would have it no other way.

As you read this book, you will learn about these women's lives through their stories, and the photographer's visual record.

The following interviews were conducted at the women's homes in 1989.

Ruth Rebecca Dewitt Middleton
1912-1992
Age at time of Interview-76

I've worked on the farm all my life. That's the best way to say it. Cause when I was four and five, right on up, see we was picking strawberries and cotton and stuff like that trying to help Mama. When I was seven years old, I was picking over a hundred pounds of cotton a day . I've picked as much as 320 pounds of cotton a day. God just give me that much a gift and see we tried to do everything we could to help Mama because it was hard **lone** then. My daddy died when I was three years old and the youngest was one year old.

I loved working on the farm. I really loved it. Now if the conditions had been some different, I probably would have went out and got me a job after I got grown and everything. But Mama was still here and her health was failing and so I just planned to just stay here with her until she died . . . so that's what I done.

Got married August 1931. It was harder during the Depression cause after the war, way back yonder, people was getting a dollar a day and then whenever Hoover got in there about '38 or something like that, it come back down you didn't get but 40 and 50 cents a day. Was a-many-a-week when I worked 50 hours for $2. A-many-a-week. That's the way it was until Hoover got in. Hoover got in in '32, I believe it was. When he got in that's when it started picking up again. I don't mean Hoover! I mean Roosevelt. He shut down everything and started all over, and that's when times started to getting better. 'Cause they was something before then! I'm telling you. They had been bad before then like when Mama was raising us up. She **won't** getting but 30 and 35 cents a day. When we come up, everything fell in line and we hope her all we could.

There was a man lived up here and he would do her **plyin'** cause she didn't have nobody to ply, and she'd do his chopping. After we got up, after Buddy (*brother*) got up big enough to ply and do, then he would do it. And around here we got an ole piece of mule and we tended a piece of land across the woods over there. I'd do the most of the plying cause I loved to ply. She'd send me and my baby brother over there to ply and I'd tell him to stay and let me ply. I'd hitch up the mule and ply all day. I'd crop tobacco. I'd hang tobacco. I've done everything just about on the farm. I've cut ditch banks. Everything on the farm to be done except work with the tractor. I ain't never worked with the tractor, but I've done all the rest of it. Won't none of it too hard to me then. It won't. I loved to do it.

We'd go in the woods and cut barn (*tobacco barn*) wood. Martha's husband would help stack it. And we'd get out there and cut fireplace wood, heater or whatever we had, stove wood, everything like that and we was usta doing that cause you see Mama had to work all the time and try to raise us and so we had to get in the wood and stuff. And we'd do it. Won't like these old sorry chillun now cause we didn't know nothing else to do and we wanted to help her. 'Cause in the wintertime she'd walk to Magnolia aplenty-of-times by herself and work all day and walk back home. And so we'd have to have in all the wood and stuff.

My oldest sister Mary, you know, she was the oldest, and she'd do the cooking and everything. The rest of us, we'd have to get in the water and wood and feed the hogs and feed the chickens and we'd do it . . . cause she couldn't do it. It would be night when she got home and she'd have to leave before day. She was working to the bulb house in the wintertime and then in summers she work the farm. At the bulb house they clean camas and caladiums. You see they growed them in the field and then they house them in the fall just like you do other fall crops…and then you set in there in the wintertime and cut the roots off and clean um up and then they box them and sell them. I worked there **a-many-a-days**. I've walked from right here a-many-a-days. . . . We'd work until around February cause we didn't work in the fields. The ones that worked in the field, why they'd work right on. . . but we'd always stop cause it was getting time for us to start picking tobacco beds and stuff like that. We wouldn't work no more 'til the next fall.

I'd like to be remembered for the life I lived and the service I give, 'cause I always **hope** sick peoples in any way I could. Mama always done that and right on up to now, I think that makes me 'bout the proudest of myself-when I'm caring for other people.

Annette Robinson Carlton
DOB: September 30, 1913
Age at time of Interview-75

I moved over here on this farm when I married. I was 16 years old. I moved in that ole house with Galloway *(husband)* and his mama, Miss Clarkie. She was nice to me. His sister Annie Lisa was pretty nice too. They knew Galloway had married a little young Girl, and they were right nice. Sis Emma (*sister-in-law*) was real good to me. But she had a house full of children and she didn't have much time. But she was real nice. She'd talk to me and tell me things. She'd teach me how to do things, too. Miss Clarkie would teach me too . . . the little that she knew.

We didn't start farming until Willie (*oldest child*) was a good big boy . . . about 7 years old. Galloway was working out to Warsaw. I've worked just like a man on this farm. Galloway would hire a lot of people to help but you'd have to work along with them. I'd have to come to the house and cook and then go back to the field with **the help** and work until night . . . sometimes way in the night. When we barned tobacco that could be work way into the night. I didn't get a chance to rest.

We've never had nothing but ole ragged fences. The cows would get out during the night and we'd have to get up and get them in. Lord have mercy. Willie and C. P. (oldest sons)…them boys worked. My last three children worked too, but nothing like the first two. I'd have to fed them boys too, cause they could eat. I'd have to get up before day and cook them breakfast and fed them and then get myself ready to go to the field whenever they went.

Them boys worked so hard. When they'd saw wood, I'd pull the cross saw while one rested and then go to the other side and pull while the other boy rested. I worked right along side them two boys. I'd try to say things to them so they wouldn't feel so bad and encourage them to do the work that their daddy had told them to do before he went to the store. I grew up along with them two boys. I'd try to have fun with them, too. Sometimes when we got an ole car, they'd be playing music on the radio and I'd go out in the yard and dance with them.

On Sunday evening after we went to church, come home and fix our little dinner, we'd just have another church almost. It wasn't church, but, we'd go to one another's house, me, Iler and Allie Bethel. We'd walk up and down the road just talking about church and one thing and the other—just have ourselves a good time walking the road and being with one another. We'd go down to Mr. Henry's cause you know Mr. Henry always loved to have fun.

At sometime during the fall if the **jersemoak** *(Jerusalem oak—a weedy North American plant having lobed leaves and a characteristic odor suggestive of turpentine)* seeds were plentiful, we'd break them and put them on a sheet and beat them out. We'd sell them. I believe they used them for medicine. The money went for the whole family. Usually we'd carry them to Sanderson's Store and he'd buy them. It was tough but I raised my children.

I'm so proud of my children. I ain't got a bad one in the bunch. I've always tried to help my children to get an education and make something of themselves. We sent them to college somehow . . . well they sent themselves. But we did what we could to help them. Willie comes out here to see about us just about everyday. When the children come in, it just gives me a lift. I've got some good children... sweet children.

Tenner Moore
1911-1998
Age at time of Interview-77

When I got married, I just moved from my daddy's farm over here. We grew corn, tobacco and cotton, and soy beans. That's about all we had. The hardest part is going in the field everyday.

Grading tobacco and stuff like that course I'd do all of that myself. Course Ivory (husband), he'd help me. I'd take it off and pile it up. That was pretty good. That's the easiest thing about tobacco. Lord, don't say nothing. Trying to put it in every week and some nights we'd have to be out in the barn or somewhere putting it in, 9 and 10 and sometimes 12 o'clock at night before we got to the house.

I was born August 30, 1911. (*Today's your birthday!*). That's the truth. I'm getting so old I forgets. Yes I'm 77 years old today. I was about 18 when I got married.

We got through the best we could. We pulled together and made it. I wasn't even 20 years old when I had my first baby. I had 11 children, one passed, so I got ten living as far as I know. We had good credit; my husband did. And we would go and get it (*necessities*) **on-time** and whenever we got the money we paid for it that way .

Talking about preserving food and stuff, Lord, I have canned butter beans, peas, apples, peaches, strawberries, plum jelly. . . some of everything I could, I'd put it in a jar and save it. What I hadn't learned from my mama *(regarding preserving food)* Ivory's mama was living then, and I learned it from her. My mama and Ivory's mama taught me to do all of these things.

I'm a Knights of Gideon. I use to go to meetings. But I don't go now. I don't go nowhere now cause I can't hardly walk, and so just stay home. They have annual turn-outs (meetings) and when one dies, I have to pay an extra dollar. But they don't give you nothing. Maggie Southerland, she collects my money and gets it in. I was in the Mothers and Daughters one while, but it went out. Well, it come to a close and I ain't been in nothing since then.

I got about 30 grandchildren. About 30 *(she counted the number of grandchildren. Her conversation and spirit lifted as she talks about her grandchildren and her children)*.

The children make me feel the proudest. Now that's the truth. I've been pretty proud of them a lot of time, but I just can't think of one specific time. Guess, I'm just glad I'm here right on, cause I could have been gone.

I need a whole lot of things. This house, it's tearing-up. It needs fixing and everything. But, I just put it out of my mind. I needs a whole lot of things. That's the truth...

I can say I've had a good life cause my daughters tries to help take care of me. If it won't for my daughters, I don't know what I would do.

Hazel Smith
DOB: August 25, 1919
Age at time of Interview-69

Some parts of the (*farm*) work we enjoyed because we worked with other people. When we'd be putting-in tobacco, we enjoyed it because we'd always be with community people. And that was kinda enjoyable. But then there were some days ...some parts of it were kinda hard, but we made it. There are some disadvantages in all work.

I remember Hoover-time. I was young but I remember it. It *(the programs of Roosevelt's New Deal)* gave some of the family work to do. It gave them a chance to get off the farm and work that little price they were paying. But children don't remember much like that.

I'd like to be remembered as honest…hard working and honest person. My service to my family and being able to stay with my children and see them out and doing things for themselves. That's important. I raised four and they're all grown. I'm about as proud of that as anything else. We were semi-prepared to have children. Of course, at that day and time there wasn't to much preparation because there weren't too many jobs to make preparation. At that time there weren't any jobs for me to do.

I enjoyed the Home Demonstration Club. I thought I would like to be with my neighbors and my friends. I enjoyed being with them. We'd have quite a good time together and it was something to do once a month—get out of the house and whatever.

It is good to live this close to my sister *(Maggie Lou Smith and Hazel Smith are sisters who married brothers and live across the road from each other).* We see each other daily. We talk with each other daily and that's good. My oldest sister is still living. She's in Mt. Olive *(N.C.).* But it is good to be close, and if anything happens we could help each other.

(She remembers her wedding day). At that time, I thought it (*marriage*) was great…a new thing. I remember it very well. It was sunny and it was bright, and clear. My dress was a flowered dress...multicolored... Often times I've heard people say, I wouldn't do this again for anything, but if I had it to do again, it would be the same cause I wouldn't know no other way to do it.

(When asked about the hot lunch program, she said.) I feel that as long as I can prepare my meals then I'm just as satisfied to eat at home. I would have to quit my work if I were busy to go out there to Warsaw to eat. So, in other words, I haven't decided to go out there to eat.

Viola Cooper Williams
1910-1996
Age at time of Interview-78

Been on a farm practically all my life. At least I can say every since I was nine years old. When I was nine years old my father died, and my mother had died when I was five years old. My father had remarried. My folks on my father's side were not farmers, and my father was a public worker. He worked **public work**—to the mills and things like that. He married the second time. When he died, she (*stepmother*) left our home in Kenansville and came back to Carlton Crossing up there with her folks. That's where we was raised at Carlton Crossing up there on the farm. That's all I had ever known. I had never worked in public work. I know how to do farm work. It's the best life in the world. Because a whole lot of people I've known have worked public work all they days and seem like they didn't prosper as much. I heard an ole gentlemen say one time, he said that he never knowed a man to buy a farm who carried a lunch bucket. And after he had said that I had turned around and kinda looked and listened. And you think back when you hear people talk. Most of the young folks now-a-days, they don't want to stop and listen when older people are talking. That's what he said. I heard it when it come out of his mouth. And I know it's kinda hard to make enough money on a public job to buy a farm.

When we first got married in 1936 we lived with his (*husband*) aunt up until December then we moved over to the Hall Farm. **Lone** in them days you could work . . . didn't make nothing. I remember the first year me and John Sammy farmed and we only cleared $25. We wanted a mill like you stuff sausage and pudding with. We bought that mill out of the $25 and we didn't have nothing left. You see we'd lived on the farm and had all that stuff we'd canned up during the summer...everything we'd saved. We had hogs. We had stuff to carry us on through the winter. We canned some of everything. Before we was able to get a pressure pot, we used the wash pot. Only thing you could get, you could get some flour and sugar because we took our corn down to Beasley's Mill and we got our bread. Things didn't cost to much. You could get five pounds of fish for a dollar, sometimes six pounds. I mean any kind of fish.

As the years grew a little better, our main goal during them days was going to church, Sunday School, and back to church. That's where you saw everybody. Get out of church and everybody would be talking, shaking hands, ha, ha, everybody would be glad to see one another. But you go to church today, it's different unless you go to church with some of them folks who come along when you come along. Things is changed.

1938. That's when I had my first child. Had a good space in there. And it wasn't so hard. It was getting a little better, cause we had everything we needed. Except, we had to get that little sugar and that little flour and we'd buy that by 25 pounds and buy a barrel of flour and set it up there in the corner and we'd have it all the winter. Didn't have to worry.

I guess I was proud when we bought this farm and built this house. Well we married in 1936. In 1947 we bought this place and built this house. Tell you what happened. The way we got this place. We would save what little money we made off of the crop, put it in the bank. We'd sell corn. We'd buy what groceries we needed. If we wanted some groceries, we'd go out to that **crib** and shuck some corn and shell it, and we were getting 50 cents a bushel for it. And I remember John Sammy borrowed a bicycle and would carry that corn out to Warsaw and sell it, maybe a bushel today and a bushel tomorrow. And then we'd pick blue—huckleberries in the woods, John Sammy would pick them just like a bird. I couldn't pick as many but I could pick some and we'd carry two crates of huckleberries out there. And we'd save that little money. We had pepper in the summer time, we'd save that little money, and we'd put it in the bank. And you know whenever we bought this place we had money enough to pay for it.

Iler B. Carlton
1912-1992
Age at time of Interview-75

Everything was cheap but money, we didn't have it. Neighbors worked together. If it hadn't been for the neighbors working with one another, I don't see how we would have made it. But they would come and help us and we'd help them. I come off the farm. That day and time every girl that married married a farmer. We grew tobacco, cotton, at that time, sweet potatoes. But you know I've always dreaded sweet potatoes. They are heavy—back-breaking job. Couldn't keep no fingernails at that time. Had rough hands the whole time we were messing with potatoes.

In the wintertime, we'd sew quilt scraps *(to make quilt tops)* for our work then. It would come kinda a warm day, we'd put in a quilt and we'd quilt that out. Had to buy batts of cotton then put it between the top and the lining and sit down with a needle and thread and sew it all the way across, making circles. We'd help each other make quilts.

We made ourselves useful through the years from one thing to the other.

(Mrs. Carlton is affectionately known as "Cousin Iler" by the scores of foster children that she has kept in her home since the mid 1960s. She recalls her days as a foster parent and one special little boy).

When Ep (husband) died, I didn't have no income. Went to Kenansville *(County Department of Social Services)* and asked if I could get two older ladies to stay with me. The woman down there said, 'why don't you keep children instead because old people are **hainty**.' I never will forget that word. How hainty they were.

Sammie--I kept Sammie a long time cause he was a little tiny baby when they brought him here and he was talking and going with me anywhere I wanted to go before they come and adopted him out. I told them *(child welfare workers)* I said you gets people to raise the younguns and get them up so they can enjoy them, I said, then you come and sell them just like you sell cows and hogs *(she laughed)*. I told them people that thing. Well, it worried me so bad. It hurt when they come and got Sammie cause you see he was so close to me and I was to him, too. Well Miss Dent called and said she didn't think the people was going to adopt him. But anyway she said, we'll bring him back this evening. Carried Sammie away that morning and said it may be this evening when we get back. I said alright, that'll be alright. They come back, about this time of evening...that same man that Sammie loved is the one that come back. He got out of the car and I said, 'Where's Sammie? He said, Miss Carlton, the people saw him and liked him and they carried him on home with them. The water went to flying. I couldn't help from crying to save me. He said, Miss Carlton, he'll be alright and probably they'll bring him back to see you. I said, 'that ain't the thing of it and you go back to Kenansville and tell Miss Dent that I said she lied! I sent word to her. She lied! Did you know them people come out here everyday for a long time—checking on me. They did. They did.

Well, I just thank God I come through it. I don't know what's wrong with peoples now. They don't have that love, cause if they had love. They say they love God, but the Bible said if you say you love Him and hate your fellow man whom you see everyday, you're a lie and the truth ain't in you. Now that's Bible. And so they just don't love. You're supposed to show your love amongst people. I ain't never minded reaching out my hand and helping somebody. Don't make no difference what race, color, Black, White, blue or green. I just reach right on in there and do it. But there are a lot who won't do that. But, I'm not looking for any credit for it.

Polly Sutton
1914-1999
Age at time of Interview-73

Lord, I've been married for 53 years, and I've been farming before then, but that's all we did. Went from one little ole farm to the other. We had it tough, but we made it somehow. We farmed on shares, every year practically all our lives, cause we didn't have no land of our own. We rented as they call it. But we had good health. I mean we didn't have too much sickness. So by that, the Lord has spared us to come this far. We raised tobacco, corn, pepper, cotton, and beans, potatoes, garden vegetables for years—all these years. We always lived in the other man's house until a few years ago, we bought this little ole house and started here. We thought it was good, cause the Lord has blessed us to be able. It beats nothing by a long way cause to think about not having a shelter for some many years—under somebody else's shelter. Didn't have no understanding. Maybe we could have started earlier, but I can say we was blessed by the merciful God.

Had four children, two boys and two girls and they lived with us 'til they got grown and went out on there own. I got married right there in the Depression, right there. We lived with his (*husband*) father about two years and helped him and had a little crop. You know how it was way back then. You just had a little bit of this, a little bit of that. When the end of the year, you were just like you was when you started. And then when you paid back what you had owed and your little half was gone and it left you with nothing. But we made it this far.

My first baby was born to 1935. At that time we stayed with Edgar's (*husband*) father and he had some young children and the young children would take care of the smaller babies to the end of the row and the middle of the field and under a shade tree. We chopped up and down those fields. *(The babies were in the field)* until my oldest girl got big enough to stay to the house and keep the baby, the younger children. We kept on farming. We hired tobacco-hands and all that—looped tobacco and put it in the barn and kept on keeping on.

Looks like we increased a little bit along as we went. We didn't get very far, but the Lord blessed us I can say. We've been making it pretty good. We ain't never been out on no public job where you could make a little money. We didn't understand to get a public job when we could have. You know how they use to go to Jacksonville and all them places, and a lot of them got a good start. But looked like we just stayed right in one place. Didn't have much education no way and that helped you a whole lot—when you had a good education. But the truth of the thing I guess we just got to going and just couldn't see no other way. So we just kept on the same old way.

Didn't have no idea what the future would bring. Cause you see that was kinda back then during the Depression. People just didn't understand and see as far as they do now. There won't nothing to be seen and different things happening that you ain't neven thought about was gonna happen. It was a long time before I even realized what the world was and that's been since television. I didn't even realize how big the world was and all these different places. I didn't realize.

I'd like to have a lot that I don't have, but I just make myself contented with what little I have cause I see all the years have done passed. I haven't accumulated all that much, but still, I just make myself content. We didn't have nothing…just ate and slept and got up and went to work.

I didn't never do no recreation. I went to church whenever I could and that's my most pleasure. Being able to go out and do the little day's toil. But far as going out to lakes and beaches, I ain't never been to a beach in my life. I don't even want to go now. Now, I'm just too old and childish and no good. I always been scared of the water anyway.

I usta go to the '**socation** *(Kenansville Missionary Baptist Association)* about every year, but I ain't been lately. But a long time ago, that was a great recreation. It was a great pleasure. And on Saturday they didn't have all these gatherings for people to go to. Poor people didn't go much. But they would look forward to going to the 'socation. It would be like a show. People would be there making pictures and they'd have little stands out to the church house, selling drinks. Your daddy had one when the 'socation was to Warsaw-First Baptist *(Church)*. I believe he had one then. But people would gather—walking from this stand to that stand, frying fish. . . that was one pleasure. Everybody went to enjoy it—walking, laughing, talking, eating, meeting different friends and so on.

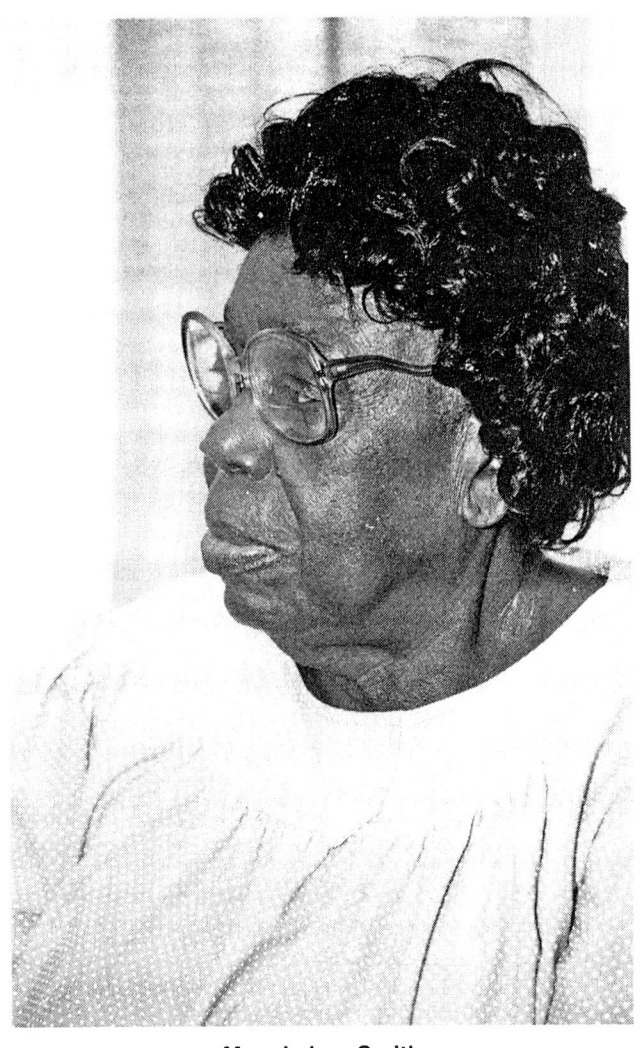

Maggie Lou Smith
1910-1999
Age at time of Interview-78

As a child, I grew up on a farm. I've been on a farm all my life. I'll say 70 years I've been farming. I married in '52. But, I've been farming all my life. I was a old-timey woman, just old-timey. I just wanted to get married to see what it was like.

The Depression was hard. It was harder then. We had ole carts and things like that. We didn't have no other transportation except a horse and buggy and a wagon or cart or something like that. In '46, I worked to Jacksonville about a year and a half or two years, but other than that, tobacco was the main crop. We had cotton, corn, and we raised a few peanuts, and cane (sugarcane). I'll never forget that. We bought flour, sugar and rice. Meal, we'd have it ground—have the corn ground down here to Beasley's Mill.

The biggest disadvantage of farming was that we won't making no money. Sho won't making no money. I was ready to work on the farm (after marriage) because there was nothing else to do. You couldn't get no job like you can now. Farming is just what you make it. It wasn't to hard to me. But, if I had it to do over I wouldn't do it.

I'm a Salem *(Grand United Order of Salem)*. I just decided to join. I wanted to be in something like that. If you get sick, they will give you a little (money). And they're supposed to come around and see about you. But, I didn't say they did. But, they are supposed to. Whenever you pass, they'll give you a little on your burial. I belong to insurances, but no other organizations.

(I would like to be remembered as) Honest, such as that. When I went to school, I believe that was just as important as anything else that I know of. I got in high school. I didn't finish, but I went about three years.

Mary Lizzie Moore
DOB: October 7, 1917
Age at time of Interview-70

I've been on this farm since 1944. In my childhood I lived on the farm. Every since we've been married we had tobacco, corn, and had some cotton, early beans, pepper and that's just about all. I have always worked in the fields and enjoy that type of work. After I got married I knew that I'd always live on the farm and I have always enjoyed it.

She remembers her wedding day. I wore a blue and white dress. We didn't have a wedding, instead we drove to Dillon, South Carolina. We have raised three children. I always liked children, so I got a chance to adopt—didn't adopt them—they was give to me and we raised them. Our oldest child was three years old when we took him. I raised my girl from age eight because I always wanted a girl. I've had good health, so far and I just love friends, love to meet friends and I love children. Just being happy—taking everything as it comes. If I could have been able to go to school—go to college and finish, I'd be proud.

The best thing about being a farm woman is that, I can work like I want to, do most anything I want to do. I go to work whenever I want to and quit whenever I want to. Always been like that. Some things have been real hard, some haven't. You know how it is on the farm. The worse thing, I guess, is whatever you try to have, whatever you tend, seems like you don't get much out of it. Some things you have right good luck with and some you don't. It's a happy life, for anybody who likes the farm. I enjoy it myself. I've always been on the farm and I just enjoy it. Anyway, I'd rather be on the farm than anywhere else.

Pearl M. Williams
DOB: December 18, 1919
Age at time of Interview-78

It was hell! I married Fred in 1929. Well, it (*the Depression*) wasn't to bad. Fred couldn't get no job laying brick so we had decided to go home and farm, but then his daddy died and he had to come and see about the farm so then we moved to North Carolina (*from Georgia*) in 1930 or 1931. We grew most of our food. Canned everything, peaches, beans, string beans, okra, squash, corn. Did I say cabbage? Cabbage—they won't fit to eat after your canned them. I believe that's about all. We killed a lot of hogs. We come here and started to raising hogs and we'd kill 10 or 11 hogs in December. Had to salt it (*the pork*) down and then wash it and hang it up in the smokehouse. I canned sausage in lard. Cooked it on the stove and then put it in the jar and then pour lard over it. It tasted right good. We sold a lot of the hog meat. Grew cotton, corn, tobacco. We had about a hundred head of chickens and we sold the eggs here in Warsaw for groceries.

I had never worked on a farm 'til we come here and then I had to cook three meals a day, feed **the help** and then go to the field—like your mama did—go to the field when they went. And then I'd be give-out, but I'd have to cook supper when I come in from work. We hired some help, cause you know, way back then we didn't have no pliers or nothing much and they had to chop the corn and you know we had to chop the cotton, and we had cane where you make syrup.

I was 21 when I got married and moved here and it didn't bother me too much and so we moved here and went to farming. I didn't know how to do nothing. I won't even no good cook yet cause Mama did all the cooking and let us do nothing and I had to learn to cook.

We had the Home Demonstration Club. I enjoyed it. That was the only time we had to get together, you know, the women. We had a good time talking and we had to make different things in the club meeting. The lady (*agent*) taught us how—how to sew and put up fruit and everything and we served a good dinner to everybody. That's what I think we went for—to eat.

Fred always wanted some more children and when I had Gloria, the ole doctor, he won't worth a toot, and he tore my womb hurrying the baby out and I didn't know it. I kept having body trouble and I'd hurt so bad trying to work (*in the fields*). When I went to have an operation, it was so bad I had to have a hysterectomy. Steven (*a family in-law*) said I believe you'd love to have Jimmy. I said yes we would (*Mrs. Williams and her daughter, then an adult, visited Jimmy several times. On a later visit Mr. Williams accompanied them.*) I said Fred do you want him and Fred said, 'Good gracious yes' We brought him home and I had made him some pajamas. Even if we didn't get him I was gonna give them to him. People say I wouldn't take no adopted child cause you don't know what they'll do. I said, you don't know what your own gone do. You read in the papers everyday where their own children kill their parents and everything . And Jimmy, he's doing real good.

(When asked what she believed her most important contribution had been, Mrs. Williams responded): Well, you know they don't do it now, but when somebody would get sick in the neighborhood, you'd go do what you could. We'd always carry food cause when Lillie Bell was sick I'd carry her food. Every time I'd cook something good, I'd go through the woods and carry it to her. When Mr. Bryant was sick, you know he had TB, I'd go set with him and he'd tell me 'don't come in here Miss Pearl cause I got TB,' and I'd fan with a piece of paper and carry him food. And when anybody died in Magnolia or somewhere, I'd always carry a lot of food and Fred would help me buy it and he just loved to carry food when they had a death in the family.

*P*art Three

Elderly Black Farm Women: A Population at Risk

Elderly Black farm women are a neglected segment of the elderly population. Their self-reliance, mutual support, and rurality have helped keep them isolated and underserved. This article describes the productive lifestyles that 10 such women in southeastern North Carolina recalled in oral-history interviews and the problems these women face because of their advancing age, poor health, caregiving responsibilities, isolation and the deterioration of traditional resources.

Elderly Black farm women are an invisible segment of the elderly population; their contributions to their families, communities and the larger society have often been overlooked. Their work and resourcefulness have been ignored because their production was generally for use, rather than for exchange. Moreover, planners, policymakers, and service providers seldom consider this group's needs when they develop policies and programs. For example, the North Carolina Aging Services Plan (North Carolina Division of Aging, 1991) only briefly acknowledged the dearth of information and lack of documented formal research about the quality of life of elderly Blacks and Native Americans and did not distinguish between the needs of women of color and White women. If elderly Black women are combined with all other elderly women or minorities, their specific needs may never be addressed within a cultural context. To its credit, the North Carolina Aging Services Plan identified obtaining information about aged minority groups in the state as a first step to serving them better. In line with this goal, it is important to understand who these elderly farm women are and how their histories have affected their current positions in society.

A search for demographic data on this population is complicated by the fact that information on minority elderly people is not usually broken down by sex and data on older women and do not include cross-classifications by minority or nonwhite status. Furthermore, demographics on farmers generally exclude this population because they have retired and their farm earnings fall below the agricultural cash-earnings cutoff of $1,000. Given these limitations the data that are available are not revealing. Nevertheless, the 1980 census reported that 603,181 North Carolina residents were aged 65 and older. In 1990, 825,377 residents, or 12.5 percent of the state's population, were aged 65 years and older. It is expected that this group will reach nearly 1.2 million by 2010. More than two-thirds of the state's older residents live in rural areas in 56 of the state's 100 counties (North Carolina Division of Aging, 1991).

Background

Duplin County, a moderately populated rural county, was the site for the current study. In 1990, more than 5,947 people, or 30 percent of that county's residents, were nonwhite. In North Carolina's inner coastal plain counties, including Duplin County, there are considerably fewer Black men than Black women aged 65 and older. Furthermore, at age 65, minority women have a life expectancy of 73.4 years. Half those who survived to be age 65 in 1980 could expect 17.3 additional years of life, and half those who were 85 in the same year could expect to live an additional 6.7 years. With the long tradition of farming in these counties, the sex ratio of women to men, and the life expectancy of elderly minority women, one can assume that more than half the minority residents aged 65 and older who are classified as rural nonfarmers in Duplin County are women who have work histories as farmers (Birdsall, Comer, Ullman, & Wilson, 1989; North Carolina Division of Aging, 1991). These data argue for the development of services and programs to ensure the health and wellbeing of this growing population of women.

Approximately three-fifths of all Black farmers in the South are concentrated in Alabama, Mississippi, North Carolina, and South Carolina. The majority of these farmers are located along the Mississippi Delta or in the bright-tobacco area of North Carolina (Schulman, Garrett, & Luginbuhl, 1985; Wadley & Lee, 1974). This research focuses on elderly Black farm women, aged 65 and older, who have spent most of their lives in the bright-tobacco area of North Carolina. Among Black farmers, the elderly constitute the largest portion of the population.

The term farmer usually refers to men, yet from information about farm families in general, it is known that women were and often continue to be a significant part of the farm communities (Bokemeier & Garkovich, 1987; Coughenour & Swanson, 1983), functioning as agricultural producers or as partners in production (Pearson, 1979). Although some studies have focused on farm women as decision makers (C. Jones & Rosenfeld, 1981; Sawer, 1973) and as performers of many specific farm tasks (Boulding, 1980; J. Pearson, 1979), they have revealed little about Black farm women. The literature search is further complicated when one searches for information on elderly Black women. An extensive literature search revealed virtually nothing about this group.

This article presents some initial insights into the lives of elderly Black farm women, based heavily on the author's illustrative interviews with elderly Black farm women, who were engaged in farm work for most of their adult lives before their retirement, and on her lifetime exposure to countless Black male and female farmers in Duplin County. The material presented is exploratory. It provides information and describes the impressions of 10 elderly Black farm women in only this one county. In semistructured, tape-recorded interviews, the author asked each woman generally about her life as a farm woman, the years of the Great Depression, her marriage (and wedding day), her needs, and the things that have given her the most pleasure and joy in life. These oral histories ran from two to more than five hours. The 10 women were selected through the snowball sampling method, that is, because they were identified by the author or by each other and because they would be willing participants.

These oral histories encouraged the women to structure their accounts and ideas of what they considered relevant and gave them an opportunity to reminisce. Through reminiscence, these women conducted a mental and oral review of their lives, and their awareness of personal strengths and a positive sense of self may have been revived. Throughout their lives, these qualities provided an impetus for their resourcefulness and mutual aid. These same qualities must be considered as programs are developed to meet this population's needs and to ensure an adequate quality of life during old age.

The author's inferences and summations are also based on her protracted and intimate relationships with this group of women. It was easy for the author to overcome many of the barriers inherent in the oral history method because she has had a lifelong rapport with the participants. The respondents trusted her to be respectful of them and of the frank and detailed content they presented and expressed confidence that she would use discretion and judgment in revealing intimate details about their lives. Although the information gleaned from this research may not be generalizable to a larger population, it is hoped that the depth of the material will offset this problem.

The Women's Relationship to Farm Production

To understand these women, it is important to understand their relationship to farm production. For these women, agricultural production primarily meant flue-cured tobacco. Historically, other crops, such as grain, fruits, or vegetables, were never major crops among Black farmers. Although cotton was the predominate crop for many years, it was replaced by tobacco. The production of tobacco lends itself to family labor and has traditionally been one of the most labor-intensive crops in the United States. The federal government intervened in the production of tobacco in the 1930s by assigning acreage allotments to landowning tobacco farmers that granted farmers the right to grow tobacco in specified areas. Acreage allotments were later replaced by poundage quotas. This change allowed the lease and transfer of allotments—poundage quotas from one farm to another within the same county. Essentially, the farmers' chances of economic success are based on their access, by ownership or rental, to a special government-controlled productive resource—tobacco allotments (Schulman et al., 1985; Wadley & Lee, 1974). The participation of Black farm women in the production of flue-cured tobacco was multidimensional and included labor roles that were linked to a larger system of allocating labor in the farm family.

According to J. Pearson (1979), farm women perform four roles in agricultural production: independent producers, agricultural partners, farm helpers, and farm homemakers. The independent producer manages the farm largely by herself. The agricultural partner shares work responsibilities and decision making with her spouse. The farm helper does not generally participate in production unless it is a busy time on the farm and extra help is needed. The farm homemaker contributes to production only indirectly by running errands and preparing food for the workers.

Few of the women interviewed could be classified as independent producers, nor did they fit neatly into the remaining three categories. Their roles as farm wives included some combination of partner, helper, and homemaker. They have been joint decision makers with their husbands in many business matters. Both their small-scale farms and their heavy commitments to tobacco production forced them to be more involved in farm operation than are women on larger farms.

On occasion, some women would "cross over" to do what was considered men's work. In describing her role on the farm, one woman took pride in her ability to do so:

"I'd hitch up the mule and plow all day. I'd crop tobacco; I'd hang tobacco. I've done everything just about on the farm. I've cut ditch bank. Everything on the farm to be done, except work the tractor, I've done."

Another woman recalled bittersweetly, "I've worked just like a man on this farm."

In addition to farm labor, these women were heavily involved in production for home consumption. Their tasks included gardening, preserving foods, and preparing meals for their family members and hired day workers. Illustrating this point, one woman recalled her role this way:

"We grew most of our food . . . canned everything, peaches, beans, string beans, okra, and cabbage.... We'd kill 10 or 11 hogs in December. We had to salt it [the pork] down and then wash it and hang it up in the smokehouse. I canned sausage in lard. We also had a hundred head of chickens, and we sold the eggs for groceries."

This woman's homemaking duties did not preclude her intense involvement in farm work. Instead, the typical practice included a combination of helper and homemaker. Her role as helper was especially intense during the tobacco-harvesting season. She described her role this way:

"I had never worked on a farm until we came here, and then I had to cook three meals a day, feed the help, and then go to the field when they [her husband and the hired workers] went. And then I'd be given out, but I'd have to cook supper when I came in from work."

Although these women were a significant part of their small-scale farm operations and actively participated in joint decision making with their husbands, clear sex-role definitions still remained. Tradition designated the man as the farmer and the woman as the helper. Janiewski (1985) noted that as the "tobacco-growing region around Durham [NC] affirmed into the late 1930s, men, not women, `toted the pocket book'" (p. 29). Women seldom questioned the patriarchal system that dictated this sexual division of labor between spouses; rather, they saw it as a complementary division of labor between spouses. Furthermore, these farm women were not involved with the mechanization of agriculture once it occurred. The women vividly recalled a much simpler and harder time when most farm work was done manually. As they gradually acquired farm equipment, such as tractors, their husbands took responsibility for operating the equipment.

These women were also excluded from another aspect of farming—deciding which crops would be planted where, which was the men's role. Likewise, the men did not participate equally in housekeeping or child rearing. Powers, Keith, and Gordy (1981) found that farmers spent less time interacting with their families than did members of any other occupational category. The Black farm women added housekeeping and child-rearing responsibilities to their other chores. One woman recalled her child care arrangements when her children were young:

"My first baby was born in 1935. At that time we stayed with my father-in-law, and he had some young children. The young children would take care of the smaller babies at the end of the row and in the middle of the field or under a shade tree. The babies were in the field until my oldest girl got big enough to stay in the house with the baby and younger children."

Attributes of Elderly Black Farm Women

These women all shared certain characteristics that allowed them to cope with the rigors of their lives as farmers. They had a strong work orientation, effective links with farm and non-farm organizations and activities, a strong family orientation, and a definite system of mutual aid.

Strong Work Orientation

All the women had a positive work orientation. They expected a life of hard work and rarely complained as they reminisced. Although they do not maintain the pace of their earlier years because of their advanced ages, they continue to work, particularly at those tasks related to production for family consumption. It is not unusual for farmers to continue to work long after many others have retired (Coward & Lee, 1985). For these women, work is such an integral part of their existence that poor health or, as they phrased it, "being no account," is the major impetus for retreating from farm labor. The following comments were typical and reflected these farm women's love of farm work and adherence to the work ethic:

"I've worked on the farm all of my life. I love working on the farm. I really love it."

"We made ourselves useful through the years from one thing to the other."

"I've always been on the farm, and I just enjoy it. Anyway, I'd rather be on the farm than anywhere else. I love the work."

For these women, work was more than a way to accomplish specific tasks for monetary or other material gain. The cooperative nature of farm work also held a strong emotional commitment that emphasized mutual affection and sisterhood.

Links With Farm and Non-farm Organizations

These elderly Black farm women were all active members and leaders in church, farm, and fraternal organizations. This finding is consistent with research findings that elderly women in general attend religious services more often, are more likely to be church members, and report a higher degree of religiosity than do elderly men (Taylor,1986). Research further shows that rural blacks attend services more frequently than do their urban counterparts and are more likely to be church members (Langford, 1974; Taylor, 1986). The rural church and the Black church have historically been significant in helping to organize the lives of their parishioners. The Black church is a place not only for worship through celebration, but for affirmation, rejoicing, and recognition (Dancy, 1977). The following comment reflects the women's general attitude toward the church:

"Our main goal during those days was going to church and Sunday school. That's where you saw everybody.... [You'd] get out of church and everybody would be talking, shaking hands ... everybody would be glad to see each other."

Membership in secret, fraternal orders was another characteristic that these women shared and that provided them with a great source of sisterhood and comradeship. The majority held membership in one or more of these groups: the Eastern Star, the Grand Order of Salem, or the Knights of Gideon. With long traditions in the Black community, these organizations provided opportunities for socializing, holding leadership positions, developing support networks, and receiving and giving mutual aid.

Eight of the 10 women were members of the same chapter of the Home Demonstration Club--a community-based organization that is part of the Agricultural Extension Service and that provides educational services to rural farm families. This organization has a long, credible history and is solidly integrated into the social fabric of the community. For these women, the monthly meetings of the club gave them an opportunity to socialize with each other and to learn better or different ways to meet their families' needs, such as preserving food, sewing, and flower arranging. The meetings also gave them an opportunity to prepare and enjoy a meal together. Several women commented that the eating together was the most enjoyable part of the meetings. Preparing and sharing food has traditionally symbolized the spiritual component of collective survival (J. Jones, 1985). In general, the club meetings reinforced the sense of sisterhood that the church initiated. They also demonstrated the women's commitment to grow and develop in their roles as farm wives and mothers.

Strong Family Orientation

Children were an essential part of these women's lives. Of the 10 women who were interviewed, only one had no biological children and had not adopted any. However, this woman lives across the road from her sister, who has four children, and has been intimately involved in the children's lives. Her living room is filled with photographs of her nieces and nephews, and she shows them off with a mother's pride. Three of the 10 women had adopted children either formally or informally. There were a total of 34 children between the 10 women.

All the women discussed their children and grandchildren during the interviews, and three of them stated that their children were their most important contribution to society. One woman who has no biological children has spent much of her time since her husband's death as a foster mother. In addition, she informally adopted a son while she and her husband were young and told the story of the neglectful teenage mother and the "sickly" infant's circumstances that led her to adopt the baby. She also formally adopted a daughter, who came into her home as a foster child. She told the following story of one foster child:

"Sammie ... I kept Sammie a long time cause he was a little tiny baby when they brought him here and he was talkin' and goin' with me anywhere I wanted to go before they came and adopted him out. I told them [the child welfare workers], I said, "You get people to raise the younguns and get them up so they can enjoy them then you come and sell them just like you sell cows and hogs" (she laughed). It hurt when they came and got Sammie cause you see he was so close to me and I was to him, too."

"Well, Miss Dent called and said she didn't think the people was going to adopt him. But anyway she said, "We'll bring him back this evening." Carried Sammie away that morning. They came back about this time of evening--that same man that Sammie loved is the one who came back. He got out the car and I said, "Where's Sammie?" He said, "Miss C, the people saw him and like him and they carried him on home with them."

"The water went to flying. I couldn't help from crying to save me. He said, 'Miss C, he'll be alright and probably they'll bring him back to see you.' I said, That ain't the thing of it, and you go back to Kenansville and tell Miss Dent that I said she lied! Did you know those people come out here everyday for a long time checking on me. They did. They did."

This is one woman's account of her love for a foster child, and its also a reflection of the commitment that all these women had toward children and family.

A majority of these women also spoke of the importance of education to success in life. They have firsthand experience with life's hardships and recognize the affliction of being Black and uneducated. They did not want their children to suffer as they had done and were determined to give their children the advantage of an education. Therefore, they encouraged their children to attend college, which for them was a major investment well worth the sacrifices and hard work involved. For several of these women, the education of their children represented the fulfillment of their own dreams of achievement. The following comment illustrates the women's general attitude toward education:

"I'm so proud of my children. I ain't got a bad one in the bunch. I've always tried to help my children to get a good education and make something of themselves. We sent them to college ... well, they sent themselves, but we did what we could to help them."

Sixteen of the 34 children attended college, and several have master's and doctoral degrees in such fields as business, education, social work, and journalism. Ironically, most of these children now live in urban centers and will probably never become farmers. Another consequence of their children's educational achievements is that they are unavailable to advocate, on a regular basis, for their aging parents.

Definite System of Mutual Aid

According to these women, group survival rests on the idea of mutual support. The women have developed a system of mutual aid and social support that has taken them through crises of family illnesses and death to general activities of farm life, such as barn raisings and hog killings. For these women, the social support network is a coping mechanism that is permanent and provides them with esteem, support, and encouragement. Preston and Mansfield (1984) found that the closeness among rural elderly people in a support network promotes feelings of security, which, in turn, help to reduce stress. Older Blacks, moreover, have not been able to count on formal support systems of service. A history of injustices, supported and often initiated by "the government," has caused elderly Blacks to develop a healthy sense of paranoia. To avoid the expected humiliation of racism that is often inherent in formal helping systems, they have established and relied on their own network of helpers. Chatters, Taylor, and Jackson's (1986) research on elderly Black people in the South showed that the "helper network" includes spouses, children, siblings, friends, and neighbors. Furthermore, Taylor (1985) found that elderly Blacks prefer to receive help from a particular group and that their help-seeking journey includes, in order of frequency, children, kin, nonkin, and formal organizations.

The elderly Black farm women in this study indicated that they often gathered for work in small groups of relatives and neighbors. Consistent with Janiewski's (1986) findings, talking and socializing was an integral part of their work. The following comments illustrate the sense of mutuality and community support inherent in their world of work:

"Some parts of farm work we enjoyed because we worked with other people. When we'd barn tobacco, we enjoyed it because we'd always be with community people. Neighbors worked together. If it had not been for the neighbors working with one another, I don't see how we would have made it. But they would come and help us, and we'd help them."

Implications for Practice

Although these women have a history as "survivors and effective copers" (Chatters & Taylor, 1989), many of the resources that were traditionally available to them no longer exist. Poor health, decreased mobility, and advancing age put their quality of life at risk. The at-risk population has been described as individuals aged 60 and older who have fewer physical problems than do the high-risk group but who experience impairment in their social, economic, mental, physical, or home and community functioning (North Carolina Division of Aging, 1991).

Elderly Black farm women are at risk in at least four important ways: economic security, health, their caregiving responsibilities, and social isolation and dependence.

Economic Security

North Carolina had the eight highest rate of poverty among the elderly in the nation for 1987, and nonwhite women aged 75 and older had the highest rate at 47.7 percent (North Carolina Division of Aging, 1991). With such a high rate of poverty, it is alarming that so few of the state's elderly people participate in any economic security programs. In 1988, for example, only 6.7 percent received Supplemental Security Income (SSI), and only 7.2 percent received food stamps (North Carolina Division of Aging, 1991). The low participation rate in such programs may be attributed to the lack of information on and understanding of these programs. Another explanation may be that the elderly fear that they will lose their land if they apply for and receive means-tested services.

These farm women can be described as land rich. Their lives have revolved around farming and agricultural activities. Although their livelihoods may not remain tied to their farming efforts, the values embodied in landownership and involvement in the community provide them with an identity, stability, and continuity (Brown & Larson, 1979). Land, according to Beaver (1982), is symbolically associated with family. The farms on which these women reside have been in their families for more than 100 years. Many can trace their land acquisitions from inheritances and small purchases from siblings or other relatives and from others. Several of the women laughingly recalled that their husbands referred to the most recently purchased parcels of land as the "new ground," although they may have been purchased 20 to 30 years ago.

Landownership gives the women not only a sense of stability but some semblance of power and control. To sell their land to younger family members or, what is less desirable, to people outside their families could devastate and dehumanize these women. Their quality of life would likely be negatively affected, both economically (with the loss of a financial base) and emotionally (in that discontinuity would probably cause undesirable or pronounced personality changes that would lead to dependence, reduced self-esteem, and depression). The very qualities that have helped these women to cope would be destroyed because low self-esteem destroys resourcefulness, self-reliance and independence.

Landownership also makes these farm women ineligible for many means-tested social programs, particularly if the land is not contiguous to their residence, which it often is not because of the haphazard method of acquiring small parcels throughout the years. Furthermore, many of these women have paid limited social security taxes and are, therefore, eligible for only small monthly social security payments. Few of them or their spouses did off-farm work and therefore, are not recipients of private pensions. Essentially, although these women have worked continuously, they are experiencing the growing poverty shared by all small-scale farmers.

In sum, the significance of this study's findings are underscored by the context of information on the financial status of elderly Black adults. The higher incidence of poverty among elderly Black individuals is a reflection of the disparity between the income levels of Black and white adults. Of the four race-sex groups (Black men, Black women, White men, and White women), black women have the lowest median income (Chen, 1985).

In dealing with the problems of economic security, social workers and other advocates for the elderly need to become more tenacious in social change efforts by lobbying for legislative changes to consolidate eligibility requirements for programs, such as food stamps, SSI, and the low-income energy-assistance program; or a system that increases the value of homestead exemptions as property values increase. The change involving the value of homestead exemptions would provide some protection to landowners and help to allay anxieties associated with landownership and the acceptance of social services.

Health

Most of the women in this study did not report chronic health problems that inhibited their functioning, but health issues were of major concern to them. The women realize that their health is tied closely to the social and economic aspects of their lives. When discussing health, they described themselves as being "no good" or "no account." In general, they suffer from physical health problems, such as vision impairments, hearing loss, arthritis, memory loss, hypertension, and stroke.

By age 65, 82 percent of Black women suffer from hypertension, compared with 66 percent of their White counterparts (B. P. Pearson & Beck, 1989). Hypertension, sometimes referred to as the "silent killer," requires early diagnosis and treatment, including a low sodium diet, which is often inconsistent with the traditional eating habits of Black farm women (Dancy, 1977). Other leading physical health problems include heart disease and stroke. Strokes are the third leading cause of death among women and hypertension is a major risk factor for stroke (B. P. Pearson & Beck, 1989). Shortly after the interviews for this study, one woman suffered a massive stroke that left her unable to care for herself. At the time of the stroke, she was the primary caregiver for an ill adult son who lived at home with her. Her concern about the care of her disabled son could further complicate her own recuperation.

Caregiving Responsibilities

Living arrangements and caregiving responsibilities present another risk factor for this group. Of the 10 women who were interviewed, only four live with their husbands. The remaining six either live alone or with someone other than a spouse. These living arrangements may mean that they have caregiving responsibilities for their spouses or for other older kin. One 76-year-old woman is living with her husband and caring for his frail elderly aunt whom she "took in." In discussing her caregiving role, she stated,

'I'd like to be remembered for the life I've lived and the service I've given, `cause I always helped sick people in any way that I could. My mama always did that and ... I think that would be `bout the proudest thing about myself ... is caring for other people."

It is not unusual for elderly women to assume caregiving responsibilities for impaired family members. Furthermore, society has come to rely on women to provide the majority of care for dependent family members who can no longer care for themselves (Wilson, 1990). In caring for others, elderly women often neglect their own health in the belief that they have no other choice but to care for those in need.

Social Isolation and Dependence

The impact of the caregiving role, along with some physical health problems, has meant that many of these women have had to give up their social and community functions. Their complaints of vision impairments and "nerves" have caused most of them to stop driving. The fact that they no longer drive, combined with the lack of public transportation in rural areas, has meant that these women must depend on others to transport them. Because they are dependent, most travel only when necessary and hence attend church less regularly. This finding is consistent with Taylor's (1986) finding that poor health and difficulty in getting around account for elderly people's decreased attendance at religious services. Furthermore, these women no longer participate in the activities of their clubs or secret orders. Although most maintain their membership in the secret orders, they do not attend meetings or other related activities. Even the chapter of their Home Demonstration Club, a source of pleasure and reward to them for more than 30 years, is now defunct. The women who were members stated that they were no longer "able" to prepare for the meetings or attend related county and regional meetings. With limited outside contact and the loss of personal freedom and mobility, these women are more dependent on their families and others for social stimulation. Hence, they are at risk of social isolation, which is an additional threat to the quality of their lives.

Aggressive outreach must form the foundation for services offered to this population, and tapping into existing rural community resources could make the process both efficient and effective (Carlton-LaNey, 1991). Because the Home Demonstration Club once served such a useful function for this group, establishing a similar in-home program under the auspices of the Extension Homemakers Association may help to provide continuity and decrease isolation. Blau (1973) noted that peer relationships, rather than filial relationships, determine morale in old age; therefore, a community-based in-home women's group could provide the women with an opportunity for information sharing and education about social services and economic security programs. Even if they are unable to retain all the information, they at least will have the advantage of knowing a resource to call upon in times of need. The group meetings could focus on a specific service each month by drawing on expertise from the local Department of Social Services (DSS), the Health Department, the mental health agency, Councils on Aging, and so on.

Given that eating together was an important aspect of the Home Demonstration Club's meetings, homemakers or chore workers from DSS could purchase and prepare light meals that are based on the club members' preferences and dietary needs. The menus of the Home Demonstration Club usually consisted of meat or chicken salads, crackers, cake, and coffee. Another option may be for the congregate-meals programs to deliver meals to the homes where the meetings are scheduled to take place. Volunteers who deliver meals to the homebound are more likely to travel to rural homes when they are delivering several meals within the same area. The spouses or other eligible individuals could also receive meals with the same delivery.

These in-home monthly meetings would be reminiscent of the pleasure that these women experienced learning and sharing with women friends in their clubs and lodges in previous years. As Berzoff (1989) noted, groups are beneficial to women who have suffered losses of self-esteem and self-worth. Furthermore, these groups provide both corrections of self-perception and ties to other women. These elderly women's clubs would be multifunctional, giving participants opportunities to interact with each other; to gain information about available services, programs, and resources; to share nutritious meals; and to develop new kinds of healing ties with other women.

Conclusion

The development and implementation of culturally sensitive programs and services requires that social workers first become aware of the culture and values of elderly Black farm women and understand and respect the ways that these women deal with problems. Social workers must also capitalize on the distinct qualities of the culture. These findings suggest that social programs and services for the elderly Black farm woman must be free of means-testing whenever possible; have an outreach component; utilize natural helpers, such as family members, neighbors, and friends; be church or community based; and be sensitive to the women's rurality, work histories, and feelings of sisterhood and mutuality. Given services that incorporate these components, elderly Black farm women will be able to enjoy old age with a heightened sense of security and a greater sense of continuity.

References

Beaver, P. D. (1982). Appalachian families, landownership, and public policy. In R. L. Hall & C. B. Stack (Eds.), Holding on to the land and the Lord: Kinship rituals, land tenure, and social policy in the rural south. (pp. 146-154). Athens: University of Georgia Press.

Berzoff, J. (1989). From separation to connection: Shifts in understanding women's development. Affilia, 4, 45-58.

Birdsall, S., Comer, L., Ullman, M., & Wilson, J. (1989). Geographic patterns of North Carolina's elderly population. Chapel Hill: University of North Carolina Press.

Blau, Z. (1973). Old age in a changing society. New York: New Viewpoints.

Bokemeier, J., & Garkovich, L. (1987). Assessing the influence of farm women's self-identity on task allocation area decision making. Rural Sociology, 52, 13-36.

Boulding, E. (1980). The labor of U.S. farm women: A knowledge gap. Sociology of Work and Occupations, 7, 261290.

Brown, M. M., & Larson, O. F. (1979). Successful black farmers: Factors in their achievement. Rural Sociology, 44, 153-175.

Carlton-LaNey, I. (1991). Some considerations of the rural elderly black's underuse of social services. Journal of Gerontological Social Work, 16, 3-17.

Chatters, L. M., & Taylor, R. J. (1989). Life problems and coping strategies of older black adults. Social Work, 34, 313-319.

Chatters, L. M., Taylor, R., & Jackson, J. (1986). Aged blacks' choices for an informal helper network. Journal of Gerontology, 41, 94-100.

Chen, Y. (1985). Economic status of the aging. In R. Binstock & E. Shanas (Eds.), Handbook of aging and the social sciences (2nd ea., pp. 641-665). New York: Van Nostrand.

Coward, R. T., & Lee, G. A. (1985). The elderly in rural society. New York: Springer.

Coughenour, C. M., & Swanson, L. (1983). Work statuses and occupations of men and women in farm families and the structure of farms. Rural Sociology, 48, 23-43.

Dancy, J. (1977). The black elderly, a guide for practitioners. Ann Arbor: Institute of Gerontology, University of Michigan.

Janiewski, D. (1985). Sisterhood denied: Race, gender, and class in a new South community. Philadelphia: Temple University Press.

Jones, C., & Rosenfeld, R. A. (1981).American farm women: Findings from a national survey. Chicago: National Opinion Research Council.

Jones, J. (1985). Labor of love, labor of sorrow. New York: Vintage Books.

Langford, C. (1974). Church attendance and city size. Journal for the Scientific Study of Religion, 13, 361-362.

North Carolina Division of Aging, North Carolina Department of Human Resources. (1991). North Carolina aging services plan: A guide for successful aging in the 1990s. Raleigh, NC: Author.

Pearson, B. P., & Beck, C. M. (1989). Physical health of elderly women. Journal of Women and Aging. 1, 149-174.

Pearson, J. (1979). Notes on female farmers. Rural Sociology, 44, 189-200.

Powers, E. A., Keith, P.M., & Gordy, W. J. (1981). Family networks of rural aged. In R. T. Coward & W. M. Smith, Jr. (Eds.), The family in rural society (pp. 421-447). Boulder, CO: Westview Press.

Preston, D. B., & Mansfield, P. K. (1984). An exploration of stressful life events, illness, and coping among rural elderly. The Gerontologist, 24, 490-494.

Sawer, B. J. (1973). Predictors of the farm wife's involvement in general management and adoption decisions. Rural Sociology, 38, 412-425.

Schulman, M. D., Garrett, P., & Luginbuhl, R. (1985). Dimensions of the internal stratification of smallholders: Insights from North Carolina Piedmont Counties. Rural Sociology,50, 251-261.

Taylor, R. J. (1985). The extended family as a source of support to elderly blacks. The Gerontologist, 25, 488-495.

Taylor, R. J. (1986). Religious participation among elderly blacks. The Gerontologist, 26, 630-636.

Wadley, J. K., & Lee, E. S. (1974). The disappearance of the black farmer. Phylon, 35, 276-283.

Wilson, V. (1990). The consequences of elderly wives caring for disabled husbands: Implications for practice. Social Work, 35, 417-421.

*P*art Four

The Last Quilting Bee

About 13 years ago, the women who lived in Crosspoint (pseudonym for a small farming community in southeastern North Carolina) had their last quilting bee. It did not require long planning or preparation. The hostess, my mother, simply made a few telephone calls to her sister/friends, asking them to come over to help her "put in a quilt." Mama had made the top of the quilt by sewing together scraps of fabric that she had acquired over time. Making quilt tops was a solitary activity, which Mama had completed before calling on her friends. There was no elaborate design; she simply wanted to be able to give a quilt to each of her daughters.

The room was prepared for her guests with the quilt stretched out, attached to a wooden frame pulled tightly and propped up on chairs stationed at each of the four corners. All the chairs from the kitchen and dining room were brought into the family room where the quilt waited. Aunt Eva, Cousin Bertha, Cousin Lucy Mac, and Miss Jewel all arrived about the same time. After greeting them, Mama apologized for the quilts not being fancy-"just something for the children." As they all took their seats around the quilting frame, Mama offered them coffee and cake. The one can of beer in the refrigerator had been saved for Miss Jewel. "She enjoys a beer," the women remarked to each other.

The quilting went on for hours with little discussion of it save a few comments about Aunt Eva's not being able to see too well and her own complaints that her "lines weren't straight." There were also comments about aching joints, weakness in the hands, and a concern that the thread wouldn't be tight enough. Together, they would periodically roll the frame inward as the quilting progressed closer to the center and would ask Mama for additional thread. Each woman had brought her own quilting needle.

The conversation brought the room to life with voices of elderly women laughing and joking but carefully listening as they worked together toward the completion of a common goal. I had no role except to wait on them, to listen, and to observe the beauty of the occasion, which I believed they felt would be their last quilting party together. They talked on for hours about their lives, joys, children, and church, with talk of their husbands as the dominant theme. They complained, reminisced, and laughed about their menfolk. Now and then, they'd slip in a little "sex talk," then, overcome with embarrassment laced with snickers, they'd look over at me and comment that they needed to shut their mouths, "with that young'un" sitting over there." The "young'un" was nearly 30 years old.

I have thought a lot more about that event during the past 13 years--not just as a daughter, niece, or cousin but as a researcher. I have come to realize the deeper meaning and implications of that quilting bee and their other activities together as neighbors, friends, child brides, relatives by marriage, and sisters through common shared experience. Their talk over the work of quilting was of as much importance as the quilt itself. During their conversations, "they shared small truths," the way that women do mainly with other women. They also actively listened to each other, reserving judgment and often leaving the "weighty" in the "hands of the Lord." Their talk was neither lofty nor intellectual. Rather, it was conversation among and between intimates. It was "real talk," the kind that reached deep into the heart, soul, and experiences of each other. It was the kind of talk that drew out the explorations, analyses, and caring from each; and each participated. They did not solve the problems of the world, nor was that their intent; rather, they reinforced healing ties among sisters.

In the 13 years since that quilting bee, the quality of life of many of these women has deteriorated, and age has brought many changes. Some have moved out of the small farming community because of illness or death of a spouse. One of the women recently died. But their love and caring for one another remain. They telephone each other occasionally. But the telephone was never the first choice for contact and was never perceived as a mechanism for visiting friends. Rather, it actually represented a barrier to the desired personal contact and hands-on experience that provided the positive reaffirmation of self these women desired. For them, "real talk" took place face to face. It was the Sunday afternoon visits that nurtured and helped to sustain them. They often speak of how much they miss each other and of how much meaning each has given to the others' lives. Because of health problems like anxiety disorders, vision impairment, and arthritis, they are less mobile and the Sunday afternoon visits have ceased, along with the quilting bees. These women have managed hard lives with help from understanding sisters; but now social isolation and loneliness are issues they must confront.

Their quilts have been passed from mother to daughter. As we, the daughters, look at or use each quilt, we are reminded of and feel the spirit of the quilting bee. That spirit represents a sense of oneness, collective identity and sisterhood for African American women, regardless of age.

As a researcher, I continue my efforts to discover and understand the "social truths" about aging women, particularly aging African American women in the rural south. Gould (1989) recommends a minority-feminist perspective as a guide to better understanding and planning for this group of aging women. This perspective involves the development of a culturally sensitive model that examines cultural differences and minority group stature jointly but "within" the context of a female experience.

The prevailing perceptions of the African American elderly must also be examined for a better understanding of this population. Current themes in gerontological literature suggest that elderly African Americans develop and use an array of coping mechanisms as well as personal and systemic resources. Essentially, elderly African Americans are perceived as effective copers and survivors (Gibson, 1986; Chatters and Taylor, 1989) who function within supportive extended family networks (Barresi and Menon, 1991; Johnson, Gibson and Luckey, 1990). Because of the mutual aid system inherent in the extended family, it is also believed that elderly African Americans in rural areas do not use formal helping services extensively (Goodfellow, 1983; Carlton-LaNey, 1991). Furthermore, religion and religious behavior are said to constitute a significant part of this populations life and coping ability (Taylor, 1986; Gibson, 1986; Haber, 1984).

Analyzing an activity like the quilting bee can help to provide some additional understanding of this group, their perceptions of work, and their perceptions of their own aging. It is significant to add that this author has had a lifelong, intimate relationship with these women. Because of my relationship with them, they were completely at ease during the research process. This essay is, therefore, based on the quilting bee as well as the author's observations of and involvement with this group of southern women over many years (Carlton-LaNey, 1989).

Several important themes about work, interpersonal relationships, and growing old surfaced from this observation and from my knowledge of this group. First, there exists a strong work orientation and commitment to work for family income and for family sustenance. Second, these farm women experience themselves in terms of relationships and connections to others. Finally, aging is viewed as a period of transition where multiple losses are coped with through prayer.

Perceptions of Work

From observing the quilting bee, one could tell that these women have always approached life in very practical and resourceful ways. Quilting was simply another form of women's work. As Miller (1984) notes, each quilt is an individual creation, although neighbors may share scraps of fabric and patterns. For most of the women of Crosspoint, quilting was done primarily to provide bedcovers for warmth during winter; essentially, it involved the production of utilitarian quilts. If the colors were bright and the patterns fancy, then perhaps the process was enhanced; but these were never prerequisites. In addition to quilting as part of rural women's work, it was also a way for these women to socialize with each other. It gave the women an opportunity to visit with each other while engaging in useful and productive work. One of the quilting women made this statement when asked about her work as a farm woman.

"In the wintertime, we'd sew quilt scraps for our work. Then it would come kind a warm day, we'd put in a quilt and we'd quilt that out. Had to buy batts of cotton . . . put it between the top and the lining and sit down with a needle and thread and sew it all the way across, making circles. We'd help each other make quilts. We made ourselves useful through the years from one thing to the other. Neighbors worked together. If it hadn't been for the neighbors working together, I don't see how we would have made it."

These women perceived of work as a communal activity. While they had many hours of solitary work, their eyes light up when they talk of farmwork with neighbors and friends. Statements reflecting regrets were infrequent. Instead, they often expressed great pride in their ability to do farm tasks well and quickly.

Harvesting tobacco was the major and most labor-intensive farm task for these women. Tobacco was the primary cash crop. Women and children typically worked at the tobacco barn "looping" the tobacco onto sticks with twine. Talk around the tobacco trucks was usually lively and enjoyable. Women often used that time to socialize younger women to acceptable and appropriate behavior, to transmit values, and to comfort and reassure each other. With regard to this specific task,one woman stated, "Some parts of [farm] work we enjoyed because we worked with each other. When we'd be putting in tobacco, we enjoyed it because we'd always be with community people."

Perceptions of Relationships

The quilting bee is an excellent illustration of peer relationships centered around a group activity. Activity theory supports the premise that activities provide the role support that is needed for the maintenance of a positive self-concept, which is correlated with high morale. Sterne and colleagues (1974) provided data suggesting, however, that friendships of African American elderly may not involve the interpersonal intimacy and the resulting role supports needed to sustain morale. Creecy and Wright (1979) concluded similarly that informal activity with friends was not associated with morale among elderly African Americans. The findings of research investigating the relationship between friendships and morale are mixed. The likelihood that, among rural elderly African Americans, the term "friend" is used loosely may help to account for the inconsistency of these findings. This assumption is supported by several research studies (Sterne, Phillips and Raushka, 1974; Creecy and Wright, 1979). On the other hand, interaction at the Crosspoint quilting bee, along with prior and subsequent observations, suggests that intimate friendships and morale are closely related. Blau (1981) supports this finding, noting that peer relationships rather than filial relationships determine morale in old age. The group of women of Crosspoint form a friendship group that functions as a social support network of natural helpers. Preston and Mansfield (1984) observed that closeness among individuals in a social network serves to promote feelings of security that help reduce stress. The Crosspoint quilting bee is one example of ways that these women took care of each other's emotional needs. It helped them to avoid social isolation and provided a time to"lighten one's personal burden" through interactions and conversations with equals. It was a time for "visiting," "catching up," and strengthening healing ties among kin.

In addition to the quilting bees, the women also gathered for their monthly meetings of the Crosspoint Home Demonstration Club. (The State Council of Home Demonstration Clubs of North Carolina, organized in 1940 and renamed the North Carolina Extension Homemakers Association in 1974, is a voluntary statewide community-based organization that is solidly integrated into the social fabric of rural America. The Crosspoint Club, now defunct, was part of this larger state organization.) Through the club these women learned new and different ways to care for their homes and families. The club, a much more formal group than the quilting bee, also gave them opportunities to socialize.

A county agent usually met with the group, facilitated the meetings, and demonstrated specific activities such as appropriate canning or sewing techniques. The meetings rotated to each member's home, and the hostess prepared a special lunch for her guests. While the women enjoyed the group learning activities, some reminisced that the meetings were one of the "few times that the women had to get together" outside of work-related gatherings. In addition to the educational component, the women of Crosspoint remembered the "eating together" and their talks during the meals as the most fun. They appreciated the input from the agent, but quickly added that they "really enjoyed themselves" when she was not present because they felt less inhibited and could enjoy each other without intrusion from an outsider. The women no longer meet as a club for the same health reasons that ended the quilting bees. Essentially, each opportunity that the women of this community had to get together strengthened their relationships and enhanced their social support network of natural helpers. These women formed a strong, natural bond of fictive kin that occurred because of proximity, necessity, and sameness.

Perceptions of Aging

The women of Crosspoint view aging as a natural and "blessed" time in their lives. It is simply a transitional period for them. As Gibson (1986) noted, aging among older African Americans is not a crisis; it is facilitated by a "well-oiled machinery" of helpers that includes a multiple use of family members and other substitute helpers. Similarly, Taylor and Chatters (1986) indicated that Southern older African Americans have larger informal helper networks than their counterparts in other regions of the country. That network includes both family and friends.

The women of Crosspoint usually speak of aging within the context of God, family, and support network. Their comments include the following:

"I thank God I can still wait on myself and my husband."

"I can say I've had a good life 'cause my daughters try to help take care of me. If it wasn't for my daughters, I don't know what I would do."

"We had it tough, but we made it somehow . . . the Lord has spared us to come this far. I can say we were blessed by the merciful God."

The "well-oiled machinery" to which Gibson (1986) refers exists for the women of Crosspoint and helps to ease their transition into old age. Their mutual aid system remains intact although some of the players are different. One Crosspoint resident recalls that her son "comes out here to see about us just about every day." Another woman who has moved out of the small farming community into a nearby town with her daughter and family smiles with pride and a sense of security when she states that she does not participate in the congregate meals program only a fraction of a mile from her home, because her son-in-law "dared" her to go, saying that he could feed her when she got hungry

Conclusion

In sum, the women of Crosspoint rely on a combination of prayer and a social support network of natural helpers to make the transition into old age. The quilting bee is an illustration of this complex support system of rural elderly African American women. Understanding such an activity can provide information useful for policy development and program planning. The quilting bee suggests, for example, that this group of women enjoy communal work and useful work. Activities perceived of as useless and solitary may get little participation. Furthermore, this friendship group of women has tended to provide empathy and a sense of connectedness for each woman. Their comments around issues of aging and health not only reflect these feelings of connectedness and interdependence, but in ways make formal helping systems seem unnecessary and unacceptable. Such perceptions may account for the paucity of services tailored to meet this group's needs. These women have learned to rely on each other for help, advice, and services. Interventions from outside must, therefore, be sensitive to being perceived as intrusive. Moreover, such interventions must be culturally sensitive and female-centered, with a carefully planned outreach component that involves familiar and valued resources like church and family.

References

Barresi, C. and Menon, G. (1991). Diversity in Black Family Caregiving. In Z. Harel, E. McKinney and M. Williams, (Eds.), Black Aged. Newberry Park, Calif.: Sage.

Blau, Z. (1981). Old Age in a Changing Society. New York Franklin Watts.

Carlton-LaNey, I. (1989). Elderly Black Farm Women as Keepers of the Community and the Culture. Greensboro, N.C.: Apple-tex Educational Center.

Carlton-LaNey, I. (1991). Some Considerations of the Rural Elderly Black's Underuse of Social Services. Journal of Gerontological Social Work, 16(1/2), 3-17.

Chatters, L., & Taylor, R. (1989). Life Problems and Coping Strategies of Older Black Adults, Social Work 34(4), 313-19.

Creecy, R. & Wright, R. (1979). Morale and Informal Activity with Friends Among Black and White Elderly, Gerontologist 19(6), 544-47.

Gibson, R. (1986). Older Black Americans, Generations 10(4), 35-39.

Goodfellow, M. (1983). Reasons for Use and Nonuse of Social Services Among the Rural Elderly, Human Services in the Rural Environment 8 (4), 10-16.

Gould, K. (1989). A Minority-Feminist Perspective on Women and Aging, Journal of Women and Aging 1(1/2/3), 195-216.

Haber, D. (1984). Church-Based Programs for Black Care-Givers of Non-Institutionalized Elders, Journal of Gerontological Social Work 7(4), 43-55.

Johnson, H., Gibson, R. and Luckey, I. (1990). Health and Social Characteristics: Implications for Services. In Z. Harel, E. McKinney and M. Williams, (Eds.), Black Aged. Newberry Park, Calif.: Sage.

Miller, J. (1984). Quilting Women, In M. Alexander (Ed), Speaking for Ourselves, New York: Pantheon Books.

Preston, D., & Manfield, P. (1984). An Exploration of Stressful Life Events, Illness, and Coping Among the Rural Elderly. Gerontologist 24(5), 490-94.

Sterne, R., Phillips, J., & Raushka, A. (1974). The Urban Elderly Poor. Lexington, Mass.: D.C. Heath.

Taylor, J. (1986) Religious Participation Among Elderly Blacks. Gerontologist 26(6), 630-35.

Taylor, J., & Chatters, L. (1986). Church-based Informal Support Among Elderly Blacks. Gerontologist 26(6), 637-42.

Glossary

A-many-a-day – often, regularly or a long period of time

Barn tobacco/put-in tobacco – means putting the harvested tobacco into a barn for curing

Boot - the trunk of a vehicle

Cane -- sugarcane

Car pocket – the glove compartment in a vehicle.

Cracklins -- are fried pieces of pork skin with attached underlying fat. They are usually served as a snack and are naturally very high in fat and cholesterol.

Crib – corn storage barn

Foley catheter – named for its inventor Frederic Eugene Basil Foley, it is a flexible plastic tube (a catheter) inserted into the bladder to provide continuous urinary drainage.

Fountain pen – ink pen

Fictive kin – people who are considered family members even though they are not related by bloodline or marriage.

Get happy – feeling spiritually moved to shout or otherwise show physical signs of emotion

Griot – (pronounced gree-oh) is the West African storyteller who perpetuates the oral tradition and history of a family, community or village. These storytellers are a repository of oral tradition.

Hainty – chiefly Southern variant of haunt, unpleasant attitude or behavior, snobbish.

Hope – past tense of help

Jersemoak – Jerusalem Oak, a sticky Old World weed naturalized in North America and having lobed leaves and an odor suggestive of turpentine.

Knee baby – refers to the next to the youngest child who is the "lap baby"

Knocked in the head – this is what happens to you when you are careless and somewhere you are not suppose to be, may also suggest bizarre behavior or unreasonable behavior

Lone – along then or during that time

New ground – most recent land purchased on the farm

On-time – buying on-time or making purchases using store credit

Phlox – small white, pink or lavender perennial wild or garden flower

Plyin' – plowing

Public work – employment off the farm, i.e., in mills or factories, etc.

Settin-up – a wake which is a traditional time period when family and friends literally stay awake or sit-up with the body of a deceased person until the funeral or burial.

'Spect – expect

'Socation -- Association

Souse – Also called souse meat or hoghead cheese. It is a jelled loaf made entirely from the meaty parts of the head of a pig. The head is cleaned and simmered until the meat falls from the bones in a liquid concentrated gelatinous broth.

The fresh – meat from a hog recently killed. Meat that has not been cured.

The help – farm workers, day laborers

Won't – wasn't, weren't

Yellow dog democrat – a staunch loyalist to the Democratic Party

About the Author

Iris Carlton-LaNey was born in Warsaw, North Carolina in 1949. She is a professor of Social Work in the University or North Carolina at Chapel Hill School of Social Work. Her research and writings have received national recognition. She received the Distinguished Recent Contributions to Social Work Education Award in 2003 from the Council on Social Work Education and was named one of the most influential social workers in the US by the University of Maryland School of Social Work. She has edited or co-edited three books.

Iris grew up on her parents' tobacco farm and is the **knee baby** of her family. She has three brothers; the oldest died in 1995 and was 20 years her senior. She has one sister. She is married to Marion L. LaNey, II, and they have one son, Marion L. LaNey, III (Donnie). She lives in Durham, North Carolina.